...ND THE AMALFI COAST

Top 10 Naples and the Amalfi Coast Highlights

The Top 10 of Everything

CONTENTS

Naples and the Amalfi Coast Area by Area

Streetsmart

Within each Top 10 list in this book, no hierarchy of quality or popularity is implied. All 10 are, in the editor's opinion, of roughly equal merit.

Title page, front cover and spine Vibrant pastel colours of the cliffside houses in Positano
Back cover, clockwise from top left Mural in Pompeii; garden at Villa Rufolo in Ravello; ruins of Pompeii; vibrant Positano houses; fjord at Furore, Salerno

Welcome to
Naples and the Amalfi Coast

From the vibrant streets of the city to sun-kissed beaches, dramatic cliff-hugging roads, ancient temples and island paradises, Naples and the Amalfi Coast is a hive of historical, cultural and natural beauty. With Eyewitness Top 10 Naples and the Amalfi Coast, the region is yours to explore.

It's hard not to fall in love with this region: the colours, the history, the beauty. What could be better than watching the sun setting across the Bay of Naples from the **Castel dell'Ovo**, uncovering historical treasures at the **Museo Archeologico Nazionale**, devouring a Neapolitan pizza hot from the oven, seeing the pastel-coloured cascade of homes in **Positano** or sipping a *limoncello* in **Amalfi**? It's all here, packed into an unforgettably beautiful landscape.

Be sure to take time during your stay to explore the cultural and artistic treasures that lie just moments from the coast. Step back in time at the ancient towns of **Pompeii** and **Herculaneum** or visit the best-preserved Greek temples in the world at **Paestum**. Escape to the island of **Capri** for spectacular natural beauty and to soak in the warm waters of the Mediterranean Sea, or get lost amidst the grandeur of the **Reggia di Caserta**. With so much to see and do, this is one of Italy's most diverse and seductive areas to discover.

Whether you're here for a weekend or a week, our Top 10 guide has all you'll need to experience everything the region has to offer, from the lively streets of **Spaccanapoli** to the panoramic vistas of **Ravello**. With travel tips throughout the guide, along with five itineraries, detailed maps and inspiring photography, this is the essential pocket-sized travel companion for your journey. **Enjoy the book, and enjoy Naples and the Amalfi Coast**.

Clockwise from top: Procida Island; Spaccanapoli, Naples; Villa Cimbrone, Ravello; bird's-eye view of Amalfi; fresco inside Villa dei Misteri, Pompeii; Blue Grotto, Capri; Temple of Hera, Paestum

Exploring Naples and the Amalfi Coast

One of Italy's most vibrantly diverse regions, Naples and the Amalfi Coast offer a wealth of artistic treasures, culture and natural beauty to discover. Here are some ideas to make the most of your stay, from an intensive weekend break in Naples to an extensive, week-long itinerary of the area.

Two Days in Naples

Day ❶

MORNING

Start in the heart of Royal Naples (see pp86–9) at the grandiose Piazza del Plebiscito. Visit the **Palazzo Reale** (see pp12–13), climb the ramparts of the **Castel Nuovo** (see pp14–15), imagine the sparkling lights at **Teatro San Carlo** (see p89) and stroll through the **Galleria Umberto I** (see p88). Stop for lunch at Brandi, known as the birthplace of Neapolitan pizza (see p93).

AFTERNOON

Revel in the vibrant atmosphere of **Spaccanapoli** (see pp76–9) and see the impressive **Duomo** (see pp16–17), majolica-tiled cloister of **Santa Chiara** (see p77) and "Veiled Christ" statue at the **Sansevero Chapel** (see p79).

Day ❷

MORNING

Step back in time at the fascinating Roman ruins of **Pompeii** (see pp30–31) or **Herculaneum** (see pp32–3). Then climb to the top of **Mount Vesuvius** (see p95) for an unforgettable view of the Bay of Naples.

Capodimonte Museum

San Gennaro Catacombs

0 metres 500
0 yards 500

From Herculaneum (15 km/9.3 miles)

Museo Archeologico Nazionale

Museo Metro Station

Duom

METRO

Sansevero Chapel

Santa Chiara

SPACCANAPOLI

METRO

Castel Sant'Elmo, Certosa e Museo di San Martino

Municipio Metro

Galleria Umberto I

Teatro San Carlo

Castel Nuovo

Brandi

Palazzo Reale

Piazza del Plebiscito

Spaccanapoli
cuts a pathway through the heart of Naples.

Castel dell'Ovo

Borgo Marinari

Key
— Two-day itinerary
— Seven-day itinerary

Clinging to the hillside, Positano is a stunning backdrop to the sandy beach.

AFTERNOON
Return to Naples to see the ancient treasures at the **Museo Archeologico Nazionale** (see pp18–21) – closed Tuesdays. Enjoy dinner in the romantic Borgo Marinari surrounded by fishing boats and the **Castel dell'Ovo** (see p88).

Seven Days in Naples and the Amalfi Coast

Days ❶ and ❷
As Two Days in Naples.

Day ❸
Head to Naples' highest district to visit the **Certosa di San Martino** (pp26–9) and **Castel Sant'Elmo** (see p89). Art lovers won't want to miss the **Capodimonte Museum** (see pp22–3) – closed Wednesdays. The **Catacombs of San Gennaro** (see p63) are also close by.

Day ❹
If desired, transfer your base to the Amalfi Coast and explore **Amalfi** (see pp36–7), with its impressive Cathedral of St Andrew and fascinating Museo della Carta. High in the mountains above Amalfi, visit the peaceful town of **Ravello** for its fine gardens and views (see pp36–7).

Day ❺
Enjoy a drive along the Amalfi Coast road from **Sorrento** (see p102) to **Salerno** (see p102), or take a ferry to soak up the sun in **Positano**, known as the "Vertical City" (see pp36–7).

Day ❻
Take the ferry to **Capri** (see pp34–5) where highlights include the famous Blue Grotto, spectacular views from Monte Solaro in Anacapri, the picturesque Marina Piccola and shopping in Capri Town.

Day ❼
Discover the ancient Greek ruins of **Paestum** (see pp38–9) and visit the excellent museum on site here.

The Greco-Roman site of Paestum contains the fascinating remains of three ancient Greek temples.

Top 10 Naples and the Amalfi Coast Highlights

Ruins of the Roman forum, Pompeii,
backed by Mount Vesuvius

TOP 10 Naples and the Amalfi Coast Highlights

This area is an anomaly – one of the earth's most beautiful and yet most accursed places. It has been the choice of the wealthy as their playground, while also being the scene of some of the greatest natural disasters. Naples itself is a vibrant urban setting, almost non-European in its intensity, while the beauty of the coast has been known to make people weep.

① Palazzo Reale

With its commanding position near the bay, the Royal Palace dominates the grandest part of the city (see pp12–13).

② Castel Nuovo

Despite its bulky towers of volcanic stone, this Renaissance castle also features one of the most graceful archway entrances of the period, carved in the purest white marble (see pp14–15).

③ Duomo

Naples' cathedral boasts a treasure-laden Palaeo-Christian basilica from the 4th century. The side chapel, dedicated to the city's adored patron saint San Gennaro, is huge and resplendent (see pp16–17).

④ Museo Archeologico Nazionale

This is the repository of ancient art that has been unearthed from Pompeii and other digs in the area. The finds evoke a Classical civilization of refinement and grandeur (see pp18–21).

⑤ Museo di Capodimonte

An unassuming hunting lodge (see pp22–3) that soon grew to become a vast royal palace. It now houses one of Italy's finest collections of art.

6 Certosa e Museo di San Martino

This museum *(see pp26–9)* that captures the true Naples. Come for peerless views, the masterpieces of the Neapolitan Baroque and the finest collection of nativity figures.

7 Pompeii and Herculaneum

The world-famous archaeological site comprises an entire culture caught in a moment when Vesuvius erupted nearly 2,000 years ago *(see pp30–33)*.

8 Capri

This small island has had a fabled history of glamour and decadence yet it still remains essentially a simple place *(see pp34–5)*.

9 Amalfi, Ravello and Positano

These three villages are a big draw along this rugged coastline known for its captivating natural beauty *(see pp36–7)*.

10 Paestum

Some of the best preserved Greek temples in the world stand in timeless splendour on this evocative plain south of Naples *(see pp38–9)*.

TOP 10 ⭐ **Palazzo Reale, Naples**

One glance at this imposing royal palace and it becomes clear that, in its heyday, Naples was one of Europe's most important cities and home to one of the Mediterranean's most glittering royal courts. Begun in 1600, it was designed by Domenico Fontana and completed in two years. Additions, including the grand staircase, were made over the years, and it was redesigned in the 18th and 19th centuries. The edifice was a royal residence until 1946, when the monarchy was exiled for its ill-considered support of Mussolini's Fascist regime.

1 Façade
Dominating the vast Piazza del Plebiscito, the palace's late Renaissance façade **(above)** of brickwork and grey piperno stone is adorned with giant statues of Naples' foremost kings.

2 Decor of the Apartments
The theme of the frescoes that adorn the 30 royal apartments was chosen to flatter royals from various houses.

3 Biblioteca Nazionale
In the eastern wing, the massive National Library has at its core the Farnese collection, with books dating from the 5th century. Also here are 1st-century-BC papyri found at Herculaneum.

4 Staircase
The monumental staircase **(left)** leads from the central courtyard up to the royal apartments. The original masterpiece dates from 1651; in 1837 it was embellished with pink and white marble.

5 Furnishings
Fine examples of Empire furniture **(above)** predominate in the palace's apartments, much of it of French manufacture. Tapestries adorn many rooms, as do exceptional examples of 18th-century marble tables, elaborately inlaid with semiprecious stones.

6 Sala di Ercole
The Hall of Hercules derives its name from the ancient statue displayed here in the 19th century.

Floorplan of Palazzo Reale

Cappella Palatina (8)

A 16th-century wooden door, painted in faux bronze, leads to the Royal Chapel **(right)**, where the court's religious activities took place. The high altar consists of semiprecious stones set in gilt copper, while the 18th-century nativity scene is a study of local life at the time.

Paintings (9)

Of considerable importance is the abundance of paintings of all genres, including works by Giordano, Guercino, Carracci, Preti and Titian. Also of interest are 17th-century Dutch portraits, 18th-century Chinese watercolours and 19th-century Neapolitan landscape paintings.

Gardens and Stables (10)

Located to the north of the palace, the gardens, which were laid out in 1841, afford great views of the hill of San Martino in one direction, and of Vesuvius and the bay in the other. The old stables here are now used for special exhibitions.

Teatrino di Corte (7)

Dating from 1768, this beautiful private theatre **(right)** attests to the royal family's passion for comic opera. In the side niches are 12 figures by Angelo Viva that depict Apollo and his Muses.

NEED TO KNOW

MAP N5 ▪ Piazza del Plebiscito 1 ▪ 081 580 81 11

Open 9am–8pm Mon–Tue, Thu–Sun (last entry 7pm)

Adm €6

▪ Caffè Gambrinus (see p93), located in a stylish piazza next to the palace, is an excellent and historic choice for a drink, delectable snacks or a full meal.

▪ The ticket office is notoriously hard to find, often confused with the gift shop. It's located on the side of the building, where the palace meets the San Carlo Opera House.

▪ It's best to buy a Campania Artecard (see p71) – it reduces entrance fees to the major sights and you will also often get prioritized entry, saving a great deal of time.

Guide to the Palazzo Reale
You are free to walk around the inner courtyard and gardens at your leisure, without a ticket, as well as to enter the National Library. To visit the Royal Apartments, buy your ticket and take the grand staircase up to the left only, after which you may see the rooms in whatever order you wish and stay as long as you like.

TOP 10 ⭐ Castel Nuovo, Naples

The Castel Nuovo is more commonly known locally as the Maschio Angioino, a name that dates the fortress's origins to the reign of Charles I of Anjou in the late 13th century. It was officially called the "New Castle" to distinguish it from existing ones, namely the Ovo and the Capuano. During the reign of Robert of Anjou, the place became an important cultural centre, attracting such greats as Petrarch, Boccaccio and Giotto for productive sojourns. It was the Spanish conquerors from Aragon who, in the 15th century, gave it its present-day militaristic look as well as Renaissance embellishments.

Architecture ①
In the 15th century five cylindrical towers were added **(right)**, as was a Catalan courtyard and the Hall of the Barons.

② Triumphal Arch
Inspired by Roman ante-cedents, the arch **(above)** was built in 1443 to celebrate King Alfonso V of Aragon and features sculpted bas-reliefs.

③ Cappella Palatina
The castle's main chapel houses frescoes from the 14th to 16th centuries, as well as a fine Renaissance sculpted tabernacle.

④ Museo Civico
On the first floor here are paintings and sculptures **(below)**, including a 16th-century *Adoration of the Magi* in which the Wise Men are portraits of kings Ferrante I and Alfonso II, and Emperor Charles V. Also here are 15th-century bronze doors, depicting royal victories over rebellious barons.

⑤ Sala dei Baroni
In 1486 Ferrante I of Aragon invited barons who were plotting against him to a ball here, where-upon he had them all executed. Today the hall is notable for its splendid vaults **(above)**.

Floorplan of Castel Nuovo

8 Paintings of Naples

The second floor of the museum focuses on Neapolitan works of a secular nature from the 18th to 20th centuries. Sculptures include *scugnizzi* (street urchins), especially the famous *Fisherboy* by Vincenzo Gemito.

9 Dungeons

Legend has it that prisoners would regularly disappear from these dungeons without a trace. The cause was discovered to be a huge crocodile that would grab their legs through a drain hole and drag them away; the hole now has a grating over it.

6 Excavations

In the left corner of the courtyard visitors can view archaeological excavations through a glass floor. Macabre surprises include skeletons of monks from an early convent on the site.

7 Views

One of the best aspects of a visit to the castle is taking in the magnificent views from its upper walls and terraces. Panoramas include Mount Vesuvius and, on a clear day, even the Sorrentine Peninsula.

FROM FORTRESS TO CIVIC PARK

The castle still retains a defensive look – most notably the sloping base surmounted by a rim of castellated battlements. In the 16th century an enclosing ring wall was added, with bastions of its own, which hid the castle from view and gave the entire area an even more ominous feel. Following Italy's Unification, however, the outer wall was demolished and the area was laid out with avenues, lawns and flower gardens, lessening the forbidding aspect of the place.

10 Inner Courtyard

This harmonious space **(below)** has typically Catalan features, such as the "depressed" arches – broader and flatter than Italian types – and an external grand staircase.

NEED TO KNOW

MAP N5 ■ Piazza Municipio ■ 081 795 77 22

Open 8:30am–8pm Mon–Sat (last entry 7pm), 8:30am–1pm Sun (last entry at noon)

Adm adults €6; between 18–24 year-olds €3

■ Inside nearby Galleria Umberto I is Sfogliatella Mary, among the best places in the city to sample *sfogliatelle*, Naples' delicious shell-shaped pastries. *(see p88)*.

■ Sometimes sections of the castle can be closed, but enquire at the information office located in the courtyard and someone may be kind enough to let you in for a quick look.

TOP 10 ★ Duomo, Naples

Naples' cathedral originally dates from the 4th century AD with the founding of the Basilica of Santa Restituta, but two centuries later the Basilica del Salvatore was built at right angles to the first and this is the site now occupied by the Duomo. Work on the Duomo as it is seen today began in the 13th century during the reign of Charles I of Anjou, but over the centuries it has suffered earthquake damages and has been restored according to prevailing tastes of the times. The result is an array of art and architecture going back 2,000 years. Next to the Duomo is the Museum of the Treasure of San Gennaro.

1 Interior and Ceiling
The interior cathedral never fails to dazzle. The floorplan is 100 m (330 ft) long, with a nave and two aisles lined with chapels (right). Sixteen pillars support arches flanked by granite columns.

2 Façade and Portals
The façade of Naples' cathedral (above) is a Neo-Gothic affair restored in the early 20th century but it is graced by three portals that date back to the 1400s.

3 Font
The cathedral's main baptismal font dates from 1618. The basin is made of Egyptian basalt, and there are Greek sculptures and an episcopal throne dating from 1376 in the right-hand nave.

4 Cappella di San Gennaro
Built in the 1600s, this Baroque extravaganza to the centre-right of the nave employed marble and precious metals and the great artists of the day to decorate its exquisite walls and domed ceiling (right).

6 Cappella Minutolo

This chapel is one of the best-preserved examples of the Gothic style of the 13th and 14th centuries. The Cosmatesque mosaic floor **(left)** and altar frescoes are of particular note.

7 Relics

The main reliquary is a gold bust of San Gennaro containing his skull bones. There is also a vial containing small ampoules of his blood.

8 Santa Restituta

Naples' oldest building was commissioned by Emperor Constantine, who made Christianity the religion of the Roman Empire. Inside are a Romanesque fresco and mosaics dating from 1322.

9 Crypt of the Succorpo

The complexity and originality of this divine Renaissance chapel have led scholars to attribute the design to Bramante.

10 Baptistry

This is the oldest baptistry in the western world. It was built towards the end of the 4th century and is adorned with splendid mosaics **(above)**. The font is thought to have come from an ancient temple to Dionysus.

5 Archaeological Area

From Santa Restituta, you can enter the archaeological area, with remnants of Greek, Roman and early Christian structures, including walls, columns, mosaics, religious buildings and Greek and Roman roads. There is some evidence of *insulae* (apartment blocks) having been here in Roman times.

SAN GENNARO

Naples' patron saint was an early Christian who battled the disapproval of Emperor Diocletian. Bent on stamping out the off-shoot Jewish sect, Diocletian set about slaughtering Christians, but Gennaro survived by his faith until he was beheaded in AD 305. His body and vials of blood were preserved in the Catacombs of San Gennaro *(see p63)* until they were moved here. Later, a believer found that his dried blood miraculously liquefied on demand, an event that became a city-wide cult.

NEED TO KNOW

MAP P1 ■ Via Duomo 147 ■ 081 44 90 97

Duomo: 8:30am–1:30pm, 2:30–7:30pm Mon–Sat, 8:30am–1:30pm, 5–7:30pm Sun

Archaeological Area and Baptistry: 8:30am–12:30pm & 2:30–6:30pm Mon–Sat, 8:30am–1pm Sun; adm €2

Museum of the Treasure of San Gennaro: 9am–4:30pm Mon–Fri, 9am–5:30pm Sat; adm €6

■ For pizza without queues, visit Pizzeria Lombardi *(see p85)*.

■ You will encounter large groups being led around by docents. No one will mind if you join the group; otherwise, take your own personal tour to another part of the cathedral until the crowds move on.

TOP 10 ⭐ Museo Archeologico Nazionale, Naples

Among the world's top museums of ancient art, Naples' Archaeological Museum overwhelms with its wealth artifacts. The building was built in the 16th century as headquarters for the royal cavalry and later turned into a museum to house the Farnese Collection and the finds that were brought to light at Pompeii and Herculaneum. Now the Farnese Collection is broken up, with the paintings at the Museo diCapodimonte and the books in the National Library, leaving this museum to focus on its ancient marvels.

4 Mosaics

Romans loved mosaics **(right)** on both floors and walls. Small chips of coloured glass and stone [tesserae] were used to create scenes of every genre.

5 Glass and Stone Vessels

Masters at producing coloured and transparent glassware, the Romans carried these techniques to artistic heights. Highlights of the collection include the celebrated Farnese Cup, engraved in semiprecious stone with layers of agate and sard-onyx, and the blue vase. Used as a wine vessel, the vase was found in a Pompeii tomb.

1 Pottery and Metal Vessels

Pottery here includes Greek and Etruscan kraters, Roman terracotta jars, vases and figurines. Grecian urns, with red figures on black back-grounds, depict a variety of scenes **(above)**.

2 Marble Sculpture

Replicas of some of the most renowned ancient Classical sculptures are housed here by artists such as Phidias, Lysippus, Praxiteles and Polyclitus. Also of great importance are the striking Greek and Roman busts.

3 Il Gabinetto Segreto

This collection showcases erotic art from Pompeii and Herculaneum. The exuberant sexuality of the ancient world inspired the frescoes, sculptures and mosaics on display.

6 Friezes, Frescoes and Murals

These Roman works **(above)** were excavated from Pompeii and disclose a great deal about the society and religion of the time.

7 Weapons, Jewellery, and Domestic Items

Shields, helmets **(right)** and swords remind us of combat, but metalsmiths also made adornments. Domestic items include lamps and cups.

8 Egyptian and Prehistoric Items

This collection, housed in the Museum's basement has art from the Ancient Kingdom (2700–2200 BC) to the Roman age. Funereal sarcophagi and mummies – including one of a crocodile – can be seen here.

BUILDING THE COLLECTION

The Farnese Collection, inherited by King Ferdinando IV from his mother in the 18th century, forms the core of the museum, including one of the most important and largest groups of Roman antiquities in existence. Excavations around Vesuvius (see pp30–31) added to the bounty. In the past 200 years the inventory of world-class treasures has been augmented by many important aristocratic collections, including the Bourbon, Borgia, Orsini, Picchianti and Astarita collections.

9 Incised Gems, Coins and Epigraphs

The collection of incised gems contains Greek and Roman pieces; bronze, silver and gold coins **(below)**, including some from Magna Graecia. Ancient written records include the *Tavole di Eraclea* (3rd century BC).

10 Bronze Sculpture

Bronze masterpieces that once adorned Villa dei Papiri in Herculaneum, including a Resting Hermes, Fauns, Water-Bearers and many statues and busts, can be seen.

NEED TO KNOW

MAP N1 ■ Piazza Museo 19 ■ 081 442 21 49 ■ cir.campania. benicultural.it

Open 9am–7:30pm Wed–Mon (ticket office closes 6:30pm)

Adm €12; €8 (EU passport holders, 18–24 years)

■ Head to Piazza Bellini and sit outside Caffè Arabo or Intra Moenia

(see p83) to gaze at the excavated Greek walls in the centre of the piazza.

■ Wheelchairs as well as tablets with video guides and Library Information Software can be obtained from the infopoint.

■ At certain times, sections may close due to ongoing excavations.

Individual Masterpieces

1 Farnese Hercules

Created and signed by Glykon of Athens, this powerful marble sculpture is a copy and enlargement of a lost bronze original by the 4th-century BC Greek master Lysippus. It was also found in the ruins of the Baths of Caracalla in Rome, where it is thought that it served as a magnificent decoration for the imperial pleasure dome. The work shows the mythical hero at rest, exhausted after having completed his round of 12 superhuman tasks. Ground floor.

2 Farnese Bull

Found in the Baths of Caracalla in Rome during excavations, this is the largest sculptural group to have survived from antiquity to date. One of the best-known pieces in the Farnese Collection, it recounts the story of Dirce (the first wife of Lykos, King of Thebes, who ill-treated Antiope and is being punished by the latter's sons by being tied to a bull. It is probably a copy – though some claim it may be the original – of a 2nd-century BC Greek work and is Hellenistic in its execution. Ground floor.

Alexander the Great mosaic

3 Alexander the Great Mosaic

Found as a floor decoration in Pompeii's Casa del Fauno, a grand aristocratic mansion of the 2nd century BC, this Hellenistic mosaic is certainly one of the most elegant and exciting to have survived. The subject is the routing of Darius's Persian armies by Alexander the Great's cavalry. The monumentality of the work is impressive and it is almost certainly a copy of a lost painting of great importance, possibly by Philoxeno. Fragmentary as it is, there are still some one million *tesserae* (tiles) in its composition. Mezzanine.

4 Dancing Faun

A more joyous image of freedom and exuberant health would be hard to imagine. This bronze was found in Pompeii's Casa del Fauno, to which it gives its name, as a decoration in the atrium to greet arriving guests. Two ancient replicas of this Hellenistic figure are known to exist; so, it must have been a popular and inspiring object. Mezzanine.

5 Hermes at Rest

Were it not for the wings on his feet, one might suppose that this very boyish Hermes (Mercury) was just a young athlete taking a break from his exertions rather than a god. The proportions of this sculpture were inspired by the work of Lysippus. First floor.

Farnese Bull sculpture

6 Sleeping and Drunken Satyrs

Satyrs to the ancients were always a symbol of pure hedonism – not just sexual licence, but every form of ease and indulgence. These two figures, from the Villa dei Papiri *(see p32)*, express a light-hearted indolence that is as implicitly erotic as it is earthy. The ancients believed that physical pleasure and delight were part of man's divine essence and gifts from the gods. First floor.

7 The Doryphoros

This is the most complete replica of the celebrated bronze original, created in about 440 BC by Polyclitus of Argos. The name means "spear-bearer" and one can see that the figure once held a spear in his left hand. It is thought to represent Achilles, and the statue was known in ancient times as the Canon, exhibiting perfect proportions in every aspect of its depiction of the human form. The sculptor developed a complex theory of measurements, related to music, for the ideal construction of the human body. Ground floor (sometimes on loan to other museums).

Prized exhibit, Farnese Cup

8 Farnese Cup

The star of the museum's cameo and incised gem collection is this glistening masterpiece, carved from a single piece of stone, specifically chosen by the artist for its layering of agate and sardonyx. The outer face of the cup has an image of Medusa; inside is an allegorical scene that probably alludes to the fertility of the Nile. The cup was produced in Egypt in the 2nd or 1st century BC. Ground floor.

Famous fresco, Sacrifice of Iphigenia

9 Sacrifice of Iphigenia

Found in Pompeii, in the so-called House of the Tragic Poet, this famous painting shows the dramatic moment when the sacrifice of Iphigenia is halted by the intervention of Artemis (Diana), who kills a deer instead. The fresco was once considered a faithful copy of a painting by the Greek artist Timante, but it is now thought to be an original Roman depiction – due primarily to its overall lack of compositional unity. First floor (can sometimes be out on loan to other museums).

10 Achilles and Chiron

Retrieved from the so-called Basilica in Herculaneum, this fresco depicts the young hero of the Trojan War with his mentor, the centaur Chiron. Since this large work was decoration for a public building, the message is clear – heed the elemental forces of Nature (symbolized by the centaur) to find balance and fulfilment in life. The image is based on a famous sculptural group, probably Greek, now lost but known to have stood in ancient Rome, as recorded by Pliny the Elder. First floor.

🔟 ⭐ Museo di Capodimonte, Naples

A royal palace, museum and porcelain factory, constructed under architect Antonio Medrano, it has been home to part of the Farnese Collection since 1759. After the French occupation in 1799, some of the collection was taken to France, but was returned following the restoration of the Bourbons. With the Unification of Italy, the palace and its treasures became the property of the House of Savoy and the residence of the Dukes of Aosta until 1947. It was opened to the public in 1957 and restored in 1996, with additions made in 1997.

1 Pre-14th- and 14th-Century Art

Most of the earliest Italian art in the museum was acquired in the 19th and 20th centuries. Important works include Simone Martini's lavish Gothic masterpiece *San Ludovico di Tolosa*.

The palace's ballroom, with its impressive chandelier

2 15th-Century Art

Powerful works here include Botticelli's *Madonna with Child and Angels* **(above)** and Bellini's sublime *Transfiguration*.

3 16th-Century Art

Here you'll find a serene *Assumption of the Virgin* by Pinturicchio, an *Assumption* by Fra' Bartolomeo and works by Titian and Raphael.

4 17th-Century Art

Strongest of all the works here is Caravaggio's *Flagellation of Christ* and Artemisia Gentileschi's horrifying *Judith and Holofernes* **(right)**.

5 18th-Century Art

Neapolitan artist Francesco Solimena is well represented here, especially by his opulent portrait of a courtier, Principe Tarsia Spinelli. Other canvases provide us with period views of Naples, its bay as well as other scenes, including one of Mount Vesuvius in eruption (above) by Pierre-Jacques-Antoine Volaire.

6 Porcelain Parlour

Designed for Queen Maria Amalia. Painted and gilded porcelain assumes the shapes of festoons, musical instruments and figurative scenes.

7 Drawings and Graphic Works

Sketches and studies by great artists are here, including works by Fra' Bartolomeo, Raphael and Michelangelo. Open mornings only.

8 19th-Century and Modern Art

History paintings and landscapes dominate this part of the collection. Endearing are the sculptures of street urchins by Vincenzo Gemito, but the signature modern work is Andy Warhol's cheerfully garish Vesuvius.

Floorplan of Museo di Capodimonte

Key to Floorplan
- Mezzanine
- First floor
- Second floor
- Third floor

9 Decorative Arts

The palace is replete with decorative arts, from ivory carvings to tapestries, to 18th- and 19th-century furniture.

10 Palazzo Reale

First conceived as a hunting lodge by Charles Barbone, the palace (above) grew into a three-storey structure.

NEED TO KNOW

MAP K1 ▪ Porta Grande Via Capodimonte; Porta Piccola Via Miano 2 ▪ 081 749 91 11

Open 8:30am– 7:30pm Thu–Tue (ticket desk closes 6:30pm)

Adm €12 (€8 for 18–24 year old EU passport holders)

Park: open 7:15am– sunset daily

▪ Choose the Museum Café for refreshment – it's located down the arcaded corridor away from the shop.

▪ The easiest way to get to the museum is by taxi. However, you can get there by bus: 178 runs from Via Toledo and R4 from Via Medina (near Piazza Municipio). From Piazza Garibaldi, take metro line 1 (to Museo) or 2 (to Cavour) and then board either the 178 or R4.

Following pages Atrani, clinging to the cliffside

TOP 10 ⭐ Certosa e Museo di San Martino

In 1325 Charles, Duke of Calabria began construction on the monastery of San Martino. The layout of the place, ensconced just below the massive Castel Sant' Elmo, is palatial, with two cloisters and an array of architectural and artistic wonders. Between the 16th and 18th century, the Carthusian monks, commissioned the greatest artists of the day to embellish their impressive edifice.

NEED TO KNOW

MAP L4 ■ Largo San Martino 5 ■ 081 229 45 02

Open 8:30am–7:30pm Thu–Tue (ticket office closes 6:30pm); Belvederes close 1 hr before sunset; Naval section closes at 2pm.

Adm €6; between 18–25 €3; under 18s free

■ The best place for delicious meal is Renzo e Lucia (*Via Tito Angelini 31/33; 081 191 71 022*). Located atop Vomero Hill, near the Certosa di San Martino, it offers a wonderful view of the city.

■ Most of the ground floor is accessible, but the upper and lower floors are under permanent restoration. If there is something you would like to see, ask one of the custodians and the locked rooms may be opened for you.

① Façade
Although originally Gothic in style, the façade **(above)** has mostly been overlain with refined Baroque decorations such as the large windows.

② Choir and Sacristy
The richly carved walnut choir stalls were executed between 1629 and 1631 by Orazio de Orio and Giovanni Mazzuoli. Take note of the cherubs and the abundance of volute curves.

③ Church
The elaborate nave of the church **(below)** is a supreme display of Baroque art and decorations – the complete record of Neapolitan art from the 17th and 18th centuries crowded into a single space.

5 Chiostro Grande

The Large Cloister has a 64-marble-columned portico designed by Giovanni Antonio Dosio. Look out for Cosimo Fanzago's marble masterpiece and the sculpted skulls, at the monks' cemetery.

THE MONASTERY'S GUARDIAN

Before entering the Certosa, be sure to take in the castle hovering above it. The monastery was built directly beneath Castel Sant'Elmo for the protection that it afforded. The original structure dates from Angevin times, but it was rebuilt by the Spanish in the 16th century on a six-pointed star design. Its original name was Sant'Erasmo, after the hill it stands on, but the name became corrupted over the centuries, first to Sant'Eramo, then Sant'Ermo, and finally to Sant'Elmo.

Beautiful view of the city from the monastery

8 Paintings and Frescoes

Dominating the ceiling is the *Ascension of Jesus* by Lanfranco, while the counter-façade has a lovely *Pietà* by Stanzione.

4 Gardens and Belvederes

One of the best aspects of the Certosa is its greenery. The views from here are picture-perfect, and the gardens themselves are lush and fragrant.

6 Chapels and Subsidiary Rooms

The eight chapels are decorated in a unified style consistent with the main part of the church. All of them are rich with brightly coloured marble and opulent gilded stucco trim.

9 Sculpture and Marble Decor

The altar, designed by Solimena, features silvered papier-mâché putti by Giacomo Colombo and angels by Sanmartino.

Floorplan of Certosa e Museo di San Martino

7 Quarto del Priore

These were the quarters of the monastery's Prior, spiritual leader and the only one of the monks who was allowed contact with the outside world. Aristocratic furnishings and priceless works of art from the Certosa collection adorn the walls.

10 Naval Section

Commemorating the Bourbon navy, this section **(above)** hosts royal barges, weapons and model frigates.

Pinacoteca and Museum Exhibits

Triptych by Jean Bourdichon

John the Baptist as a Child. Its twisting composition, with St John kissing the Child's foot and Mary looking on, embodies tenderness.

4 Baroque Art

This era is the collection's strongest suit. Significant sculptures include a *Veiled Christ* in terracotta by Corradini and a devout Lanfranco painting, *Madonna with Child and Saints Domenico and Gennaro*, is typical of the age.

1 Early International Renaissance Art

The most outstanding piece here is a triptych by Jean Bourdichon of the Virgin and Child and saints John the Baptist and John the Evangelist (c.1414). The work employs masterful perspective and anatomical detail.

2 Early Italian Renaissance Art

Of special note here is a 15th-century view of Naples, the *Tavola Strozzi*, by an unknown artist and the first painted view of the city from the sea.

3 High Renaissance Art

The most significant works here are marble sculptures, including a late 16th-century work by Pietro Bernini, *Madonna with Child and St*

5 Jusepe Ribera

The great Spanish artist, who worked in Naples for most of his life, was appreciated for his dramatic style (see p45). His *St Sebastian* is one of the most powerful works, showing the ecstatic face of the young man, his body pierced with arrows.

Bernini's *Madonna with Child*

6 Micco Spadaro

This artist's *Martyrdom of St Sebastian* provides an interesting contrast with Ribera's work. Rather than focusing on the man in close-up, he is shown off to the right being tied up, just before Roman soldiers let their arrows fly. Another Spadaro work shows the monks of the Certosa thanking Christ for sparing them from the plague, with a view of Naples' bay through the arcades.

***Tavola Strozzi*, a 15th-century view of Naples from the sea**

Floorplan of Pinacoteca and Museum Exhibits

Key to Floorplan
- Ground floor
- First floor

7 Stanzione

Stanzione's *Baptism of Christ* is noteworthy for the luminous way the flesh is rendered, employing pronounced effects of *chiaroscuro* (light and shade).

Nativity scene, Cuciniello Presepe

8 Nativity Collection

Of all the priceless nativity scenes and figures here, the Cuciniello Presepe is by far the most elaborate. Quite lost is the manger scene amid 180 shepherds, 10 horses, 8 dogs, folk going about their business, a Moroccan musical ensemble and much more. Lighting effects create dawn, day, dusk and night.

9 Glass, Porcelain and Gold

The objects here go back to the 1500s and includes painted plates, vases, tiles, pitchers, mirrors and figurines. Subject matter ranges

NATIVITY SCENES

The custom of nativity scenes is traditionally traced to December 1223, before a sculptured group of the Holy Family flanked by a live ox and ass. However, in 1025, there was already a church of Sancta Maria ad Praesepem in Naples, where a representation of the Nativity became the focus of devotion.

Called *presepio*, derived from the Latin *praesepe* or "feeding trough", referring to the Christ Child's initial resting place, the art of the nativity scene grew to become a major undertaking in the 1600s. Kings and queens would vie with each other to gather together the most impressive, dazzling, poignant and often humorous display, commissioning the best artists and designers of the day. It was not until the end of the 19th century that these wonderful works were fully recognized as an artistic genre in their own right.

The oldest example of a monumental Neapolitan *presepio* comes from the church of San Giovanni a Carbonara; sculpted by Pietro and Giovanni Alemanno in 1478–84, it originally included 41 life-size wooden figures, of which 19 still survive in the church.

from religious, such as a coral and gold Crucifix, to mythological, to scenes from daily life.

10 Neapolitan 19th-Century Art

Pre- and post-Unification was a time when Italians awoke to their cultural heritage and began to capture it in art. City views and its environs are informative of bygone days, as are the portraits.

🔟 ⭐ Pompeii

Two thousand years ago, few people knew that Vesuvius was a volcano, although in AD 62, what turned out to be a premonitory tremor caused damage to the coastal town of Pompeii as well as to other towns in the vicinity. Years later, residents were still repairing the damage to their homes and public buildings. Then, in AD 79, came the most devastating eruption. Horrific as it was for those who suffered, the result was the preservation of an ancient culture like a time capsule to be discovered centuries later.

Forum **1**
Every Roman city centred commercial, civic, political and religious life around the Forum **(right)**, generally a long rectangular area.

2 Amphitheatre
Far to the east stands Pompeii's amphitheatre – a typical oval shape, though small by Roman standards **(above)**. It was the first of its kind to be built for gladiatorial combat.

3 Stabian Baths
To the west of Via Stabiana are the Stabian Baths, dating back to 4th century BC. The stuccoed vaults in the men's changing room have preserved images of nymphs and cupids.

4 Theatre
The large theatre, built in 2nd-century BC in the style of the Greek system, used the slope of the land for the *cavea* (seating area).

5 House of Menander
This grand house **(above)** includes an atrium, peristyle and baths. It proved to be a treasure-trove of silver objects, now on display in Naples' Museo Archeologico.

6 Brothel
The *lupanarium*, which is the largest of the ruined Roman city's brothels, is decorated with frescoes depicting erotic, sometimes explicit, acts, which help to give some clue to the proclivities of the prostitutes.

Map of Pompeii

300 metres
(328 yards)

V. D. VESUVIO
VIA DI NOLA
VIA DELL'ABBONDANZA
VIA DI CASTRICIO
V. D. FORTUNA
VICOLO DI VANE EUROPA
V. D. FORO
V. STABIANA
PIAZZA
ANFITEATRO

V IV III XI VII II VIII

⑦ House of the Vettii

One of the most beautiful houses in Pompeii, the interior is adorned with splendid paintings and friezes featuring mythological themes.

⑧ House of the Golden Cupids

This sumptuous house was named after the gold-leaf decorations of *amorini* (cupids) in the bedroom. It was owned by the Poppaea family, that of Nero's second wife. The gardens were adorned with sculptures, marble tables and a pool.

⑨ House of the Faun

The 1-m (3-ft) bronze statue of the Dancing Faun **(left)**, found here in the middle of the court-yard pond, accounts for the name of this house, which covered an entire city block. Wall decorations and *opus sectile* mosaic marble floors can be seen here.

⑩ Via dei Sepulcri and Villa dei Misteri

The Way of the Tombs lies outside the city gates for fear of the dead bringing bad luck. Outside the city walls is the rustic, 90-room House of the Mysteries, where you can peek in to see the marvellous wall paintings.

MOUNT VESUVIUS

In ancient times, Vesuvius was simply "the mountain", covered with vegetation and vines, until it famously blew its stack in AD 79. At least five other occurrences have been recorded in the last 400 years and experts estimate that it could erupt again at any time. Its last rumble was in 1944, when the pointed cone disappeared, along with the smoky plume that issued from it.

NEED TO KNOW

MAP E4 ▪ Via Villa dei Misteri 2 ▪ 081 857 53 47 ▪ www. pompeiisites.org

Open 9am–7:30pm daily (to 5pm Nov–Mar); last entry 90 mins before closing time

Adm: €13

Herculaneum, Oplontis and Stabiae: 8:30am–7:30pm daily; Herculaneum €11; Oplontis €7; cumulative ticket available €22

Villa dei Papiri: 9am–noon Sat–Sun; must book ahead at www. arethusa.net

Crater of Vesuvius: 9am–5pm daily (to 3pm Nov–Feb; to 4pm Mar & Oct); adm €10

▪ There are on-site cafés at Pompeii and Herculaneum.

▪ Guided tours are also available – call 081 857 53 47.

▪ Some houses may be subject to closure due to restoration work.

Herculaneum, Oplontis and Stabiae

1 Villa dei Papiri

The remains of the resort town of Herculaneum were discovered before Pompeii but were harder to excavate since it was covered by a thicker layer of volcanic ash. Fortunately, this also meant that every aspect was better preserved. This villa was one of the first to be explored, housing art treasures now in the Museo Archeologico *(see pp18–21)*. The papyrus scrolls that give the villa its name are in the National Library.

Map of Herculaneum

(25 km/ 15.5 miles)
(750 metres/ 820 yards)
(15 km/ 9.3 miles)

CORSO RESINA
DECUMANUS MAXIMUS
VIA MARE
DECUMANUS INFERIOR
CARDO VI
CARDO V
CARDO IV
CARDO III
Ticket Office
Entrance

Art uncovered at Villa dei Papiri

2 House of the Stags

The name derives from the sculpture of stags being attacked by dogs that was found here. Other sculptures include a Satyr with Wineskin and a Drunken Hercules.

3 House of the Mosaic Atrium

This house takes its name from its mosaic floor of black-and-white geometric patterns. Gardens and rooms with views of the sea must have made it a lovely place to relax.

4 Stabian Villas

Set on the Varano Hill just outside Castellammare di Stabia, both villas preserve mosaic floors, gardens, peristyles and frescoes. Villa Arianna is named after a fresco of Ariadne being abandoned by Theseus. Villa San Marco sports a gymnasium, pool and interesting frescoes.

5 Trellis House

This building provides a wonderfully preserved example of what an ordinary multi-family dwelling was like. Two storeys high, it has a balcony that overhangs the pavement and its walls are composed of wood and reed laths with crude tufa and lime masonry to fill in the frame.

6 House of Neptune and Amphitrite

This is named after the mosaic of the sea god and his nymph-bride that adorns the fountain in the summer dining room at the back of the house. Other fine mosaics can be seen here too. The shop attached to the house has wooden structures and furniture in perfect condition.

The eponymous mosaic, House of Neptune and Amphitrite

Mosaic decoration, City Baths

7 City Baths

Built in 10 BC, these traditional baths are fascinating. They are divided into male and female sections, both decorated with the same sea-themed mosaics featuring tritons and fish. At the centre of the complex is an open porticoed area used as a gymnasium.

Marble counter tops, Thermopolia

8 Thermopolia

The Thermopolia is an example of a fast-food outlet of the day. The terracotta amphorae set into the marble counter top would have contained various comestibles. Only wealthy people had facilities to cook food, so most would stop by such a place to eat.

9 House of the Wooden Partition

A kind of "accordion" partition here was devised to separate the atrium from the *tablinium*, the room of business affairs.

THE ERUPTION OF AD 79

On 24 August AD 79, Mount Vesuvius suddenly erupted. The apex of the calamity started at about 10am and by 1pm it was all over – all the cities on the mountain's slopes were covered with lava, and Pompeii and its citizens were entirely buried. It lay undiscovered until 1750.

Here are the words of Pliny the Younger, who survived to write an eyewitness account of the events: "On Mount Vesuvius broad sheets of fire and leaping flames blazed at several points, their bright glare emphasized by the darkness… an ominous thick smoke, spreading over the earth like a flood, enveloping the earth in night… earth-shocks so violent it seemed the world was being turned upside down… the shrill cries of women, the wailing of children, the shouting of men… Many lifted up their hands to the gods, but a great number believed there were no gods, and that this was to be the world's last, eternal night…The flames and smell of sulphur… heralded the approaching fire …The dense fumes… choked… nearly everyone, to death."

10 Villa of Sabina Poppaea and Villa of Crassus

These beautifully preserved aristocratic villas, buried during the eruption of Vesuvius, are located in what was once the ancient resort of Oplontis. The complex includes gardens, porticoes, private baths, a pool and astounding wall decorations.

TOP 10 ⭐ Capri

Ever since ancient times, this luxuriant, saddle-shaped rock in the Bay of Naples has captured the world's imagination as a place where dreams can be realized and life can become an earthly paradise. Hopes and wishes notwithstanding, the island does have something special, perhaps generated by its sheer dramatic beauty, its crystal-clear waters and its lush vineyards and lemon and olive groves that seem to cover every available corner.

Marina Grande ①
Whether by ferry, hydrofoil or private yacht, virtually all visitors to the island arrive at this little port town – a mesmerizing sight as you approach **(right)**. It's a colourful place, but the bustle is only skin-deep – in reality it's just as laid back as the rest of Capri.

Capri Town ②
Piazza Umberto I, which is known simply as "Piazzetta" **(above)** is the town's outdoor salon, filled to the brim with chic bars and restaurants. Nighttime is when the true Capri denizens come out to play.

Villa Jovis ③
Emperor Tiberius's 1st-century-AD villa, built on the cliff's edge, is now in ruins **(right)** but the views of the Bay of Naples, from the highest point at this end of the island, are dazzling.

Arco Naturale ④
Follow signs from Capri Town for this easy-going walking trail, where rocky staircases offer fine panoramas of the mainland coastline. The Natural Arch itself consists of a huge limestone crag, jutting out and with the bright turquoise sea seen below.

Via Krupp and I Faraglioni ⑤
Via Krupp **(above)** is a switchback path carved into the cliff face. From here there are views of I Faraglioni rocks.

Marina Piccola ⑥
This small harbour has private bathing huts, a pebbly arc of beach, wonderful rocks for diving from and several good fish restaurants.

7 Monte Solaro

No trip to the island is complete without a chairlift ride up to Capri's highest peak, from which you can look down on the pastoral timelessness of lemon groves, little white houses, and endless flower gardens that cover the island – breathtaking.

8 Anacapri and Punta Carena

Before 1877, when the road was built, Anacapri was isolated and is still less pretentious than the rest of the island. From here, another great jaunt is to the lighthouse at Punta Carena, where a rocky beach, as well as good facilities and restaurants awaits.

9 Villa San Michele

Built by a Swedish doctor on the site of one of Tiberius's houses, Villa San Michele is an eclectic mix of Romanesque, Renaissance and Moorish styles, surrounded by gorgeous gardens.

A GLAMOROUS PAST

Capri emerged on the upmarket tourist map in the 19th century, but the high point of famed "Gay Capri" was the early 20th century, which is when it began to attract literati such as Norman Douglas, Graham Greene, Somerset Maugham and Maxim Gorky. Later on, the 1960s, the era known as "Capri People", brought the international jet-set to the island, which included *La Dolce Vita* swingers, Hollywood film stars, and even the beautiful newly-wed Jacqueline Kennedy.

Map of Capri

10 Blue Grotto

The island's most famous attraction is this sea-grotto, of a colour and intensity of blue that can be experienced no-where else **(left)**. Local oarsmen ferry visitors inside – be aware that the grotto can close at short notice due to tide levels.

NEED TO KNOW

MAP C5 ■ Tourist Information: Piazzetta Cerno 11, 081 837 06 86, www.capritourism.com

Ferries and hydrofoils leave from many ports, including Mergellina and Molo Beverello in Naples, Sorrento, Positano, Amalfi, Salerno, Ischia and Castellammare di Stabia.

Journey times to Capri: 80 mins from Naples; 40 mins from Sorrento. Hydrofoils take half these times.

■ In Capri town there are many good eating and drinking options in and around Piazzetta.

■ To get a feel for the island, take one of the recommended hikes – or better still, rent a kayak and go exploring along the otherwise inaccessible coastline areas.

■ Note that Villa Krupp can often be closed for safety reasons.

⭐ Amalfi, Ravello and Positano

With its dramatic coastline dotted with villages clinging to cliffs that drop down to the azure sea, the beauty of the Amalfi Coast has been luring travellers since ancient times. Beyond the striking landscape lies a fascinating history in Amalfi, home to the powerful Republic of Amalfi in the Middle Ages. Positano's idyllic setting and pastel-hued homes draped with fauna leave an indelible mark, while Ravello is set boldly upon a rocky spur, suspended high above the sea.

① Duomo di Amalfi

Sitting atop a staircase, Amalfi's cathedral **(below)** is dedicated to St Andrew and features the 13th-century Cloister of Paradise, museum, crypt and sumptuous Baroque interior.

② Museo della Carta, Amalfi

Discover Amalfi's important role in the history of papermaking at this interesting small museum *(see p49)*, which is evocatively set in a historic paper mill.

③ Valle delle Ferriere, Amalfi

Hike from Amalfi into the Valle delle Ferriere (Valley of the Mills) where ruins of once prosperous paper mills are surrounded by a lush forest.

NEED TO KNOW

MAP E5 ■ Tourist Information: Amalfi, Via delle Repubbliche Marinare, 089 87 11 07; Ravello, Via Roma 18, 089 85 70 96; Positano, Via Regina Giovanna 13, 089 87 50 67

Villa Cimbrone: Via Santa Chiara 26. 089 85 74 59. 9am–sunset daily. Adm €7

Villa Rufolo: Piazza del Duomo. 089 85 76 21. 9am–30 min before sunset daily. Adm €7

Duomo di Ravello: Piazza del Duomo. 089 85 83 11. Church 9am–noon, 5–7pm daily, museum: 9am–7pm (summer), 9am–6pm (winter) daily. Adm €3

Duomo di Amalfi: Piazza Duomo. 089 87 13 24.

9am–1 hr before sunset daily. Adm €3

Museo della Carta: Via delle Cartiere 23. 089 830 45 61. 10am–6:30pm daily (summer), 10am–4pm daily except Mon (winter). Adm €4

Santa Maria Assunta: Via Marina Grande. 089 87 54 80. 8am–12pm, 4pm–8pm daily

4 Atrani

Amalfi's next-door neighbour to the east is the picturesque fishing village of Atrani **(below)**, which is one of Italy's smallest municipalities. The narrow alleys and main square are a flash-back in time and the beach is an attractive alternative to Amalfi's.

5 Scala

This tiny hamlet, built on a succession of terraces, is well worth a visit for the outstanding views it affords when you look back at its larger neighbour, Ravello.

Map of Amalfi and Ravello

- 5 Scala
- 8
- 7
- Ravello
- Pontone
- 6
- 2
- Atrani
- 1
- Amalfi
- 3
- (10 km/6.2 miles)
- 9 10

6 Villa Cimbrone, Ravello

The creation of an English lord, Ernest Beckett, the house imitates the Moorish style that predominates in Ravello, and its gardens are set with Classical temples **(above)**.

7 Villa Rufolo, Ravello

The 800-year-old Arab-style palace and its lovely terraced gardens **(above)** have inspired lots of visitors. The terrace is used in summer for staging concerts.

8 Duomo di Ravello

The 11th-century cathedral is a treasure-trove of works. Its beautiful pulpit (1272) has twisted columns resting on sculpted lions at the base.

RAVELLO MUSIC FESTIVAL

Each summer Ravello is transformed into a haven for music lovers. The concert (www.ravello festival.com) offerings range from chamber music to opera, dance, jazz and world-class contemporary performers. The festival was inspired by Richard Wagner and Edvard Grieg, the 19th-century composers who were moved by the natural beauty, gardens and views of Ravello. For the most part, concerts and events take place at Villa Rufolo and the Auditorium Oscar Niemeyer.

9 Santa Maria Assunta Church, Positano

With its multi-coloured majolica-tiled dome and shimmering white and gold Baroque interior, Positano's main church is as pretty as its setting.

10 Fornillo Beach, Positano

Follow the scenic pathway hugging the cliff to this beautiful beach set in a cove flanked by two watchtowers; the perfect respite from the summer crowds.

🔟 ⭐ Paestum

Paestum enjoyed 1,000 years of prosperity, first as Greek Poseidonia, founded in the 7th century BC, then under the Lucanians, then the Romans. But the crumbling of the Roman Empire led to the gradual abandonment of the city and with that, the degradation of the fields, which turned into malaria-ridden swamps. No one dared come near the spot until the 18th century when Charles III of Spain was having a road built; trees were cut down, and there they were – three intact Greek temples. Much more was discovered in the 20th century.

1 Walls
At its peak, Paestum was large and prosperous, as evidenced by its impressive 5 km (3 miles) of walls, set off with towers and gates at strategic points.

2 Basilica
The oldest temple on the grounds, from c. 530 BC, was most likely dedicated to two deities, Hera and Zeus.

4 Amphitheatre
This Roman structure dates from the 1st century BC or later, and is only partially excavated, the rest lying under the 18th-century road, but some of the exposed part has been rebuilt. Its capacity was small – only about 2,000 – compared to others in the region.

5 Temple of "Ceres"
Votive offerings found here suggest that this small temple, further north than the other sites, was actually dedicated to Athena.

3 Temple of "Neptune"
The last of the three temples to be built at Paestum, in about 450 BC, is also the finest and the best preserved **(above)**. It may have been dedicated to Neptune (Poseidon), but some scholars argue for Apollo, and others for Zeus.

6 Museum
This informative museum exhibits finds from this excavation and several important ones nearby **(left)**. One of those sites is the Sanctuary of Hera Argiva, built by the Greeks at the mouth of the River Sele in about 600 BC. There is a collection of Roman finds upstairs.

7 Tomb Frescoes

Most famous of the exhibits in the museum are the tomb frescoes **(above)**. Virtually the only examples of ancient Greek painting to survive, they are full of light and bright colours.

8 Sculpture

Prime examples in this category of the museum include archaic metopes (decorative architectural elements) and one of two dancing girls from the Sanctuary of Hera Argiva, so well carved in bas-relief that each of the figures seems to be moving in space.

9 Pottery

Fine examples of Grecian urns are on view, including a krater with red-figured painting on black, depicting a young satyr and a girl reluctant to succumb to his blandishments, and an amphora with black figures on red celebrating the fruit of the vine.

10 Artifacts

Other artifacts here include a bronze vase that contained honey, amazingly still liquid at the time it was found due to unique atmospheric conditions below ground.

Map of Paestum

MAGNA GRAECIA

Being great seafarers, the ancient Greeks were indefatigable colonizers. Each important city-state sent out expeditions all over the Mediterranean to set up new cities. Magna Graecia (Greater Greece) formed the southern part of the Italian peninsula, along with Sicily, which the Greeks dominated for centuries, until the Romans expanded their hegemony. Paestum (Poseidonia) was one such Greek city, as were Naples (Neopolis), Cumae, and many more.

NEED TO KNOW

MAP H6 ▪ Via Magna Graecia 917 (SS18)
▪ www.museopaestum. beniculturali.it

Open 8:30am–1 hr before sunset daily; Museum: 8:30am–7:30pm daily (to 1:40pm first & third Mon)

Adm €7 for site, €4 museum, €9 for both

Tourist Information: Via Magna Graecia 887; 0828 81 10 16 ; www.infopaestum.it

▪ Frequent buses run from Salerno to Paestum; at least three buses run daily from Naples – visit www.fs busitaliacampania.it – or take the train to Paestum Station (1 km/ half a mile from site).

▪ There are plenty of snacks and light meals available up and down the tourist strip.

▪ To see the temples at their most evocative, visit at dawn or at dusk.

The Top 10
of Everything

**Naples' imitation of the Pantheon,
San Francesco di Paola**

🔟 Moments in History

1 Greek Colonization

From the 8th to the 5th centuries BC this southern area became an important part of Magna Graecia when Greek city-states set up trading posts here *(see p39)*. In 470 BC Neapolis (New City) was founded, which later became modern Naples.

Norman king, Roger II

2 Vesuvius Erupts

Around 326 BC the area was absorbed into the Roman Empire and by the 1st century AD Naples was a renowned centre of learning. But in August AD 79 all that changed when Mount Vesuvius suddenly erupted after centuries of dormancy. Within a few hours, entire cities were gone, covered by ash or boiling volcanic mud *(see pp30–31)*.

3 Byzantine Siege

With the fall of the Roman Empire in the 5th century, the area was overrun by tribes from the north, particularly the Goths. In 553 the Byzantine emperor Justinian's chief general Belisarius conquered the zone.

4 Norman Conquest

In 1140 the Norman king Roger II made his triumphant entry into Naples – the Normans had already gained possession of Sicily and most of southern Italy. The once proudly autonomous city now had to take a back seat to Palermo – although wellbeing continued to rise, due to the Normans' stability and efficiency.

5 Angevin Capital

In the mid-13th century, the French Anjou dynasty, having taken over the Kingdom of Sicily, shifted its capital to Naples *(see pp14–15)*. Many new buildings were erected, including, in 1279, the Castel Nuovo.

6 Sicilian Vespers

With the removal of the capital to the mainland, Sicilian resentment came to a head on Easter Monday 1282. A riot, known as the Sicilian Vespers, left 2,000 Frenchmen dead and initiated a 20-year war. Finally, Sicily was lost and the Angevin kings focused their attention on Naples, leading to great prosperity.

Sicilian Vespers riot

Giving thanks after the plague

7 Plague of 1656

At the beginning of the 17th century Naples was Europe's largest city, but in 1656 a plague struck. After six months, three-quarters of the people were buried in mass graves.

8 King Charles III Enters in Triumph

In 1734 the Spanish king arrived in Naples. He was heir to the Farnese clan, who were Italian by birth, and transformed his new home town into a city of the Enlightenment.

Garibaldi's arrival in Naples

9 Naples Joins a Unified Italy

On 21 October 1860 Naples voted to join a united Italy, under the rulership of an Italian king, Vittorio Emanuele II – Garibaldi had entered the city two months previously to gather support.

10 Le Quattro Giornate Napoletane

On 27–30 September 1943 Neapolitans showed their true character. After the occupying Nazis threatened to deport all the city's young males, rioting by the populace kept the Germans so busy that the Allies were able to get a toehold and rout the enemy.

TOP 10 HISTORIC FIGURES

1 Parthenope
The siren spurned by Ulysses gave her name to the first Greek colony, in 680 BC, now Pizzofalcone.

2 Spartacus
This runaway slave led a revolt of the oppressed from headquarters on Vesuvius.

3 Romulus Augustulus
The last emperor of Western Empire died in Naples in AD 476.

4 Belisarius
The general was sent by the Byzantine Emperor to reconquer much of the Italian peninsula in the 5th century.

5 Pope Innocent II
When the Normans were making progress towards Naples in 1137 the city turned to the pope for help, but the Normans took him prisoner.

6 Queen Joan I
Joan (1343–81) was so loved by the people that they forgave her for plotting the murder of her husband.

7 Tommaso Aniello
This fisherman led a revolt in 1647 against the taxation policies of the Spanish rulers.

8 Maria Carolina of Austria
The sister of Marie Antoinette was the power behind the throne of her husband, Ferdinand IV (1768–1811).

9 King Joachim Murat
Napoleon's brother-in-law ascended the throne of Naples in 1808 but was executed in 1815.

10 Luigi di Magistris
Naples' current left-wing mayor has been credited with spurring the past decade's civil and social renaissance.

Maria Carolina of Austria

🔟 Churches in Naples

Santa Chiara's majolica cloister

1 Santa Chiara
The original church here was built in 1310 and, after various renovations, it has been returned to its glorious Gothic style (see p77). The most famous feature is the adjoining convent's 18th-century majolica cloister.

2 San Francesco di Paola
A rarity in Naples, this Neo-Classical structure imitates the Pantheon (see p87), Rome's great pagan temple to the gods built in the 2nd century AD. Inside and out the basilica is austere, with the exception of the polychrome marble Baroque altar that has many statues.

3 Duomo
The oldest wing of Naples' cathedral (see pp16–17) is the city's most ancient surviving building, a Paleo-Christian church dating from the 4th century. The cathedral also has the oldest baptistry in the western world, with glorious mosaics. Archaeological excavations here have revealed structures reaching as far back as the ancient Greeks.

4 Monte di Pietà
MAP P2 ■ Via S Biagio 114
■ Open 9am–7pm Sat (to 2pm Sun)
This majestic building and its adjoining church were built in the late 1500s as a charitable institute set up to grant loans to the needy. In return, the noblemen who provided this service were granted eternal salvation. Decorated mostly in late-Renaissance style, inside there are sculptures by Pietro Bernini and frescoes by Corenzio.

5 Santa Maria Maggiore
MAP N2 ■ Via dei Tribunali
■ Open 9am–1pm Mon–Sat (adjacent chapel only)
Nicknamed *Pietrasanta* (holy stone) after its ancient stone marked with a cross, thought to grant indulgences to whoever kissed it, the original church here was built in the 10th and 11th centuries and the bell tower is Naples' only example of early medieval architecture. The present church, however, is Baroque.

San Francesco di Paola, dominating Piazza del Plebiscito

6 Pio Monte della Misericordia

MAP Q2 ■ Via dei Tribunali 253 ■ 081 44 69 44/73 ■ Open 9am–2pm Thu–Tue

This charitable institution was founded in 1601, inspired by Counter-Reformation precepts which gave weight to such works as a way of ensuring salvation. The church is set back from the street by a five-arch loggia, where pilgrims could find shelter. The altarpiece, *The Seven Acts of Mercy* by Caravaggio, is an allegory of charitable deeds. Upstairs is an art collection.

Ceiling fresco, Certosa di San Martino

7 Certosa di San Martino

This sparkling white monastery complex (see pp26–7) commands the most perfect location in the entire city, attesting to the wealth and power the monks once enjoyed. In the 17th and 18th centuries they commissioned the greatest artists of the day to embellish their church and chambers in Baroque style – the church, in particular, is a flamboyant catalogue of colour and pattern, sporting at least one work by each and every famous hand of the age.

8 Santa Lucia

MAP N6 ■ Via Sta Lucia 3 ■ 081 764 09 43 ■ Open 8am–noon, 5–7:30pm daily

According to a legend, a church stood here in ancient times, but experts date the earliest structure to the 9th century. Destroyed and rebuilt many times, the present church is postwar. The artworks were destroyed during World War II, save an 18th-century statue of St Lucy and two paintings.

9 San Pietro ad Aram

MAP R2 ■ Corso Umberto I 192 ■ Open 8am–noon, 4–6:30pm Mon–Fri; 8am–noon Sun

Tradition holds that St Peter celebrated his first mass in Naples here. The church is 12th-century, but an early Christian church and catacombs were unearthed in 1930.

10 Santa Maria del Parto

MAP J2 ■ Via Mergellina 21 ■ Open 4:30–8pm daily

The Neapolitan poet (and humanist) Jacopo Sannazaro, ordered this church to be built in the 16th century and his tomb behind the high altar is notable for its lack of Christian symbolism. In a side chapel the painting of the Archangel Michael searing the "Mergellina Devil" records the spiritual victory of a bishop when a woman proclaimed her love for him.

🔟 Piazzas and Fountains

① Piazza Plebiscito, Naples

MAP M5

This vast, magnificent urban space has been restored to its original grandeur. On one side is the church of San Francesco di Paola (see p87), and on the other the Palazzo Reale (see pp12–13). The royal equestrian statues on the square are all the work of Canova.

Fontana dell' Immacolatella

② Fontana dell' Immacolatella, Naples

MAP K2 ▪ Via Partenope, near Castel dell'Ovo

Composed of three triumphal arches, this Santa Lucia district landmark once adorned the Palazzo Reale. It dates from 1601 and is another creation of Pietro Bernini, as well as Michelangelo Naccherino. This grand fountain stands at one end of the seafront Lungomare

(see p54), while the Sebeto Fountain, a later work by Cosimo Fanzago, marks the other terminus.

③ Fontana del Nettuno, Naples

MAP P4

Shifted from its home at Piazza Bovio in 2001, the beautiful Fountain of Neptune now graces a wide spot on Via Medina. The 16th-century masterpiece is the work of three artists, including Pietro Bernini.

④ Piazza Bellini, Naples

Without a doubt, this is central Naples' most charming square (see p79). With inviting café tables lined up on the sunny side and elegant architecture facing all around, Piazza Bellini is a favourite spot for intellectuals, artists, students and anyone who wants to take a break.

⑤ Piazza Dante, Naples

MAP N2

Following Italian Unification, a statue of the poet Dante was placed in the centre of the broad curve of this square, which was accordingly renamed. Before that, the area was known as Largo del Mercatello, when it was a major marketplace. Today it is still a busy focal point of the old part of the city.

Dante's statue, Piazza Dante

Piazza San Domenico Maggiore
MAP N2

Named after the massive church that towers above the square, this piazza is flanked on three sides by impressive 17th-century palaces and adorned with an elaborate obelisk.

Piazza Duomo, Ravello
MAP E4

A visit to Ravello should begin in this charming piazza, as there are a number of different routes you can take from here. Staircases and ramped walkways lead off in all directions.

8 La Piazzetta, Capri

Magnetic at any time, this is Capri's most popular spot *(see pp34–5)*. Marked by a domed bell tower, it has many cafés with tables outside, surrounded by whitewashed arcades.

La Piazzetta, Capri

9 Piazza Tasso, Sorrento
MAP D5

The bustling heart of Sorrento, this piazza is the focal point of daily life. Find a spot at a café surrounding the square to take it all in. Constructed over a deep ravine, the square is named after the 16th-century poet Torquato Tasso from Sorrento. From the piazza, a steep road leads down to Marina Piccola, where ferries arrive and depart.

10 Piazza Duomo, Amalfi
MAP E5

Dominated by the steps up to the cathedral and the black-and-white design of the building and its bell tower, this square is a hub of café life.

TOP 10 PARKS AND GARDENS

Gardens of Augustus, Capri

1 Gardens of Augustus, Capri
MAP C5 ▪ Via Matteotti
▪ Open dawn–dusk daily ▪ Adm
The island's primary green spot.

2 Orto Botanico, Naples
The "Royal Plant Garden" was founded by Joseph Bonaparte in 1807 *(see p79)*.

3 Real Bosco di Capodimonte, Naples
Established by Charles III, this vast royal park boasts numerous ancient trees *(see pp22–3)*.

4 Villa La Floridiana, Naples
These grounds have been a public park since the 1920s *(see p60)*.

5 Villa Comunale, Naples
This large public park is famous for its statuary and fine structures *(see p88)*.

6 Parco Virgiliano, Naples
This hilltop position provides fine panoramas *(see p111)*.

7 Caserta Park, Naples
These 18th-century gardens were influenced by Versailles *(see p113)*.

8 La Mortella, Ischia
MAP A4 ▪ Via F Calise 39, Forio
▪ Open Mar–Nov: 9am–7pm
Tue–Thu, Sat–Sun ▪ Adm
Ischia's fabulous gardens include rare species.

9 Santi Marcellino e Festo Cloister, Naples
MAP P3 ▪ Largo S Marcellino 10
▪ Open 9am–1:30pm; 2:15–4:30pm
Mon & Thu
The site of former 8th-century monasteries enjoys fine views.

10 Villa Cimbrone, Ravello
Many agree that the view from Villa Cimbrone is the most beautiful in the world *(see p37)*.

🔟 Museums and Galleries

Eighteenth-century Nativity scene, Certosa e Museo di San Martino, Naples

① Certosa e Museo di San Martino, Naples

This monastery *(see pp26–9)* complex is home to several collections of art. The Pinacoteca, comprising part of the Prior's Quarters, is notable for its works from the Renaissance and Baroque eras, many commissioned for the monastery. On the upper floors, 19th-century works convey the look and feel of Naples during Italian Unification. A section devoted to Nativity scenes demonstrates the power and beauty of this Neapolitan art form.

② Museobottega della Tarsialignea, Sorrento

MAP D5 ▪ Via S Nicola 28 ▪ 081 877 19 42 ▪ Open Apr–Oct: 10am–6:30pm daily; Nov–Mar: 10am–5pm daily ▪ Adm

Sorrento is known for its fine inlaid wood furniture and objects *(intarsio)* and this museum is devoted to the delicate art. The collection is housed in a beautiful restored palace.

Inlaid wood desk at the Museobottega della Tarsialignea

③ Museo Archeologico, Naples

An insurpassable museum for Greco-Roman art *(see pp18–21)*, with important pieces unearthed in Rome and in towns around Vesuvius. The experience is a total immersion in the life of the ancients – their religious beliefs, sports, eating habits, and even their erotic peccadilloes.

④ Museo di Capodimonte, Naples

This world-class museum *(see pp22–3)* also owes its main masterpieces to the Farnese Collection. Paintings run the gamut from medieval to contemporary; the porcelain collection also shouldn't be missed.

⑤ Pinacoteca Girolamini, Naples

MAP P2 ▪ Via Duomo 142 ▪ Open 8:30am–7pm Tue–Thu (to 1pm Sat & Sun) ▪ Adm

For Neapolitan Baroque lovers, this little-known gallery is a must. There are fine works by Caracciolo, Vaccaro, Giordano and Ribera.

6 Museo Nazionale della Ceramica Duca di Martina, Naples

MAP J4 ■ Via Cimarosa 77
■ Open 8:30am–7pm; closed Tue
■ Adm ■ www.coopculture.it

Naples is famous for fine ceramic production. This museum displays exquisite Italian pieces by Capodimonte and Ginori artisans, plus creations by the factories of Meissen, Limoges, Sèvres and Saint-Cloud. Majolica works, from medieval times and a ceramic collection from China and Japan, dating back to the T'ang dynasty is also on display.

7 Museo della Carta, Amalfi

Set in a paper mill, this museum preserves one of Europe's oldest papermaking factories. In addition to the original stone vats and machinery there's also an exhibit which traces the history of the paper industry.

8 Museo Diego Aragona Pignatelli Cortes, Naples

MAP K6 ■ Riviera di Chiaia 200
■ Open 8:30am–5pm Wed–Mon ■ Adm

Built in 1826, the villa was donated to the state in 1952 by Prince Diego Aragona Pignatelli's granddaughter. The loveliest rooms are the red hall, furnished in Louis XVI style, the smoking room with leather-lined walls and the ballroom with its mirrors and chandeliers. Also of particular interest is the Coach Museum. Today, the Villa Pignatelli often plays host to temporary exhibitions and concerts.

9 Museo Archeologico di Pithecusae, Ischia

MAP A4 ■ Corso Angelo Rizzoli 210, Lacco Ameno ■ 081 99 61 03 ■ Open 9:30am–1:30pm; closed Mon ■ Adm

Housed in the 18th-century Villa Arbusto, exhibits illustrate the history of ancient Ischia. Many objects date back to the 8th century BC. Among the most famous pots found at a nearby necropolis is a typical late geometric *krater*, depicting a shipwreck scene.

Exhibit at Museo Archeologico, Paestum

10 Museo Archeologico, Paestum

Among this museum's treasures (see pp38–9), are ancient Greek tomb paintings that were only discovered on the site in 1968. Other finds include bronze vases, terracotta votive figures and various funerary furnishings.

TOP10 Artists and their Masterpieces

Crucifixion (c.1308) by Pietro Cavallini

1 Pietro Cavallini

Many scholars now credit this Roman artist (c.1259–c.1330) with much of the St Francis fresco in Assisi, formerly attributed to Giotto. Cavallini's work in Naples includes *Scenes from the Lives of Christ and John the Baptist* in San Domenico Maggiore (*see p80*).

2 Donatello

The *bas-relief* of the Assumption, the cardinal's head and the caryatid on the Right of the Tomb of Cardinal Rinaldo Brancaccio in Sant'Angelo a Nilo church (*see p80*) are assumed to be the only pieces that exist in Naples by this Florentine master (1386–1466).

3 Masaccio

A 15th-century *Crucifixion* by this Tuscan painter (1401–28) is one of the treasures of the Capodimonte Museum. The work is a blend of the formal medieval tradition and the vitality of the Renaissance. Of note are the anatomical accuracy of Christ's torso and the sense of drama created by the outstretched arms of Mary Magdalene.

4 Caravaggio

This Baroque master (1571–1610) created a lasting artistic revolution with his dramatic use of light and shade. He spent a year or so in Naples; among the works `he completed here is *Flagellation of Christ*, originally in San Domenico Maggiore but now in Capodimonte.

5 Titian

This consummate painter of the Venetian Renaissance (c.1448–1576) is represented in Naples by several works, all but one in the Capodimonte Museum. These include his sensuous masterpiece *Danaë*, and the religious works *La Maddalena* and *Annunciazione*.

6 Sandro Botticelli

Typical of this much-loved Florentine artist (1445–1510) is his *Madonna with Child and Two Angels* in the Capodimonte Museum. Although it is an early work, all of the hall-marks of the painter at his height are here: the delicacy of the veils; the refinement of features; and the soulful eyes, evoking sublimity.

Madonna with Child and Two Angels (c.1465) by Sandro Botticelli

7 Domenichino

A mammoth fresco cycle by this painter (1581–1641) adorns the Duomo's Cappella di San Gennaro *(see p16)*, depicting episodes from the life of Naples' patron saint.

8 Jusepe Ribera

The Spanish painter (1590– 1652) spent much of his life in Naples, where he created powerful and original works. These include his *San Sebastiano* in the Certosa e Museo di San Martino *(see p28)*.

9 Artemisia Gentileschi

It is said that Gentileschi (1593–1652) was violated in her youth and brought the pain of her indignation to her astounding *Judith and Holofernes*, now in Capodimonte. She was virtually the only female artist of the age to rise to fame.

Triumph of Judith by Luca Giordano

10 Luca Giordano

One of the most prolific of Naples' Baroque artists (1634–1705). His paintings and frescoes are ubiquitous in the city, adorning churches and museums. Most significant is *Triumph of Judith* (1704) on the Treasury ceiling in the Certosa di San Martino *(see pp26–9)*.

TOP 10 WRITERS AND PHILOSOPHERS

St Thomas Aquinas

1 Virgil
The epic poet (70–19 BC) lived in Naples for many years, incorporating local legends into his work *The Aeneid*.

2 Petronius
In his saga *The Satyricon* (only a fragment survives), this author (d. AD 66) captures the decadence of the Roman Empire in the villas of Naples.

3 Pliny the Younger
Thanks to this writer (AD 62–113) we know much about the day Vesuvius erupted and buried Pompeii *(see p33)*.

4 Suetonius
The writer (AD 70–126) is famous for his *Twelve Caesars*, scandalous accounts of the first Roman emperors.

5 St Thomas Aquinas
The theologian (1225–74) was often a guest at San Domenico Maggiore, headquarters for religious study at the University of Naples.

6 Petrarch
The great lyric poet and scholar (1313–74) often visited the court of Robert of Anjou in Naples.

7 Giovanni Boccaccio
Author of *The Decameron* (1348–53), 10 tales of ribaldry in medieval Naples.

8 Torquato Tasso
Tasso was an epic poet and a native of Sorrento (1544–95).

9 Giovanni Battista Vico
Born in Naples, Vico (1668–1744) found fame with his influential *La Scienza Nuova (The New Science)* published in 1725.

10 Benedetto Croce
The philosopher, historian and statesman (1866–1952) spent much time in Naples.

TOP 10 Icons of Popular Culture

Pulcinella figurines, Naples

1 Pulcinella
Cunning, perpetually hungry and rambunctious, Pulcinella (Little Chicken) is the symbol of Neapolitans and their streetwise way of life. His signature white pyjama-like outfit, peaked hat and hook-nosed mask go back to ancient Roman burlesque, in which a bawdy clown, Macchus, was one of the stock characters. He is the prototype of Punch and similar anarchic puppets around the world.

2 Presepi
The tradition of creating sculpted tableaux of Christ's birth (presepi) has risen to a high art in Naples ever since the 1700s. Many sculptors create scenes that expand far beyond the central event and include features of everyday life – Pulcinella might be represented slapping the current mayor, for example.

3 Sophia Loren
An indefatigable love goddess since her star began to rise in 1957 in L'Oro di Napoli (The Gold of Naples), "La Loren" went on to become a Hollywood star.

Sophia Loren

4 Scugnizzi and Lazzaroni
These two characters, products of the poverty the city has historically suffered, are street urchins and ruffians. Both have been heavily romanticized by outsiders, yet their sly wisdom and wit are traits all Neapolitans seem to aspire to.

5 Neapolitan Song
Naples has always been known as a city of music, with songs focusing nostalgically on love, the sun and the sea. O' Sole Mio and Santa Lucia are the most renowned.

Un Turco Napoletano, starring Totò

6 Totò
This rubber-faced comedian was the quintessence of Italian humour. Until his death in 1967, "The Prince of Laughter" made five films a year, some of them comic master-pieces, including Un Turco Napoletano (A Neapolitan Turk, 1953).

7 Pino Daniele
Known as the voice of Naples, Pino Daniele was one of Italy's most popular singer-songwriters. He was known abroad for his songs Quando and Je so pazz. After his death, a street in Naples was named in his honour.

8 Massimo Troisi
Embodying the heart of the Neapolitan character, this actor made international waves with *Il Postino (The Postman)*, nominated for an Academy Award in 1995. Sadly, after the film was completed, Troisi died at the age of 41.

Massimo Troisi

9 Naples in the Movies
Greats of the golden age of Italian cinema all felt inspired to communicate their impressions of Naples. Notable films include Roberto Rossellini's *Viaggio in Italia* (1954) and Francesco Rossi's *Mani Sulla Città* (1963).

10 Recent International Films and Series
Naples and the coast have provided the setting for films as diverse as the fifth *Star Wars* instalment, partly shot at Caserta's Royal Palace, Anthony Minghella's *The Talented Mr Ripley*, partly shot on the islands of Procida and Ischia, and the HBO series *My Brilliant Friend*, based on the popular novels by Neapolitan author Elena Ferrante.

A scene from *The Talented Mr Ripley*

TOP 10 OPERA LEGENDS

Gaetano Donizetti

1 Teatro San Carlo
The oldest continuously working opera theatre in Europe is a UNESCO World Heritage site (*see p89*).

2 Inauguration
On 4 November 1737 the San Carlo was inaugurated with Metastasio's opera *Achille in Sciro*.

3 Castrati
An 18th-century Neapolitan speciality, renowned *castrati* included Farinelli (Carlo Broschi) and Gian Battista Velluti.

4 Fire
A February 1816 fire destroyed the San Carlo. In a few months the theatre had been rebuilt with perfect acoustics.

5 Ballet
San Carlo shares with La Scala the record for the first Italian ballet school (1812).

6 Gioacchino Rossini
The composer was artistic director of the opera house between 1815 and 1822.

7 Gaetano Donizetti
Donizetti composed 16 operas for the San Carlo.

8 Vincenzo Bellini
In 1826 Bellini staged his first work at the San Carlo, *Bianca e Gerlando*.

9 Giuseppe Verdi
The "god" of Italian opera wrote his first opera for the theatre, *Alzira*, in 1845.

10 Enrico Caruso
Arguably the most famous tenor ever, Caruso was born in Naples in 1873.

TOP 10 Romantic Spots

1 Villa Cimbrone, Ravello

Greta Garbo enjoyed her love affair with the conductor Arturo Toscanini in this lovely spot *(see p36)*, declared by American writer Gore Vidal to be one of the most beautiful places on earth. Wander the maze-like gardens over terraced levels; the highlight is the Terrace of Infinity, with breathtaking views.

Terrace of Infinity, Villa Cimbrone

2 Villa La Floridiana, Naples

MAP J4 ■ Via Domenico Cimarosa 77 ■ Open 8:30am–2pm (to 7pm in summer)

Lucia Migliaccio, Duchess of Floridia, once called this sumptuous place home – a love token from her husband, Ferdinand I, whose morganatic wife she became soon after the death of his first wife, Maria Carolina of Austria. Not only is the story romantic but the situation itself affords some of the finest views of the city and the bay. The gardens are an excellent place for a peaceful stroll,

and the main building now houses a museum filled with a number of delightful treasures *(see p47)*.

3 Ristorante Da Adolfo, Positano

MAP E5 ■ Via Laurito 40 ■ 089 87 50 22 ■ €€

Hidden away in a tiny cove just east of Positano is the tranquil Laurito beach. Since 1966, this beachside restaurant has been serving freshly caught fish, mozzarella grilled on lemon leaves, and locally made wine with fresh peaches. The restaurant offers free boat service for clients from Positano's main pier and the ride is five minutes long. Sunbeds and umbrellas are available to rent, so arrive early for a romantic day at the beach.

4 Le Sirenuse, Positano

In the heart of Positano, Le Sirenuse *(see p131)* has earned its reputation as one of the most romantic hotels on the Amalfi Coast. Even if you're not a guest, you can enjoy an unforgettable meal with a view at the Michelin-starred La Sponda restaurant.

Balcony at Le Sirenuse, Positano

8 Villa Eva Resort, Anacapri

Set amid subtropical gardens, this resort *(see p128)* consists of a main house and bungalows. Each accommodation is unique and there's a wonderful grand piano-shaped pool.

9 Garden of Augustus, Capri

MAP U2 ■ Via Matteotti ■ Closed mid-Nov–Feb ■ Adm

The views from the Gardens of Augustus makes Capri one of the most romantic spots *(see p35)*. The gardens are perfect for admiring the Faraglioni rocks, zigzagging Via Krupp and mesmerizing turquoise sea.

5 Marechiaro

This fishing village between the tip of Capo di Posillipo and Punta del Cavallo *(see p111)* is famous with locals for its romantic atmosphere. The vista from here is said to be so gorgeous that even the fish come here to woo their sweethearts by the moonlight. There are many excellent restaurants around the prime viewing spot, all specializing in fish.

6 Monastero Santa Rosa, Conca dei Marini

MAP E5 ■ Via Roma 2 ■ 089 832 11 99

This secluded former monastery *(see p130)* is the dream hotel for a romantic escape on the Amalfi Coast. Wander hand in hand through the terraced gardens or enjoy a dip in the beautiful infinity pool.

7 Le Grottelle Restaurant, Capri

MAP U1 ■ Via Arco Naturale ■ 081 837 57 19 ■ Closed mid-Nov–Mar, Tue (not Jul–Aug) ■ €€€

The cuisine here is simple, homemade fare that includes seafood, pasta, chicken and perhaps rabbit, while the wine is local and very creditable. What makes it so romantic is the setting. Not only is it close to nature, situated near the Arco Naturale, but the terrace tables also enjoy an eye-popping view straight down to the sea, along a precipitous ravine. In addition, the friendly owners do their best to make any meal a memorable event.

Garden of Augustus, Capri

10 Villa Maria Restaurant, Ravello

MAP E4 ■ Via Sta Chiara 2 ■ 089 85 72 55 ■ €€€

Such a beautiful view from the vine-covered garden deserves superb food, and that is just what you find here. The restaurant, part of the Hotel Villa Maria *(see p130)*, is one of Ravello's best, specializing in fresh fish and seafood as well as local wines; try the incredible lemon mousse.

Following pages Santa Maria Assunta Church, Positano

TOP 10 Beaches

One of many beaches on Procida

1 Procida
This small island has several good beach options (see p102). One of the longest stretches from Chiaiolella Marina to Ciriaccio, called the Lido, is the island's most popular beach so expect crowds. From here a bridge leads to the nature reserve of Vivara, which has rocky access to the sea. To the northeast, Pozzo Vecchio also has a beach.

2 Posillipo and Beyond
MAP J2
The nearest beaches to the centre of Naples that are of any appeal can be found at Posillipo, although most are shingle, not sand, and the water isn't quite immaculate. Further away, at the ends of the Cumana and Circumflegrea railways, there are more attractive sandy beaches, although, again, they are not entirely pristine.

3 Sorrento
In this resort town, bathing platforms have been constructed, with lifts or steps leading down to them from several

hotels (see p102), but unless you are a hotel resident you will have to pay for this option. Elsewhere along the peninsula there's a fine beach to the east, at Meta di Sorrento, while to the west, there's a small sandy beach at Marina di Puolo and another at Marina di Lobra.

4 Capri
There's very little in the way of sandy beaches here, although there are small ones around Marina Grande. (see pp34–5) A popular pebbly choice is Marina Piccola, where facilities include restaurants. The adventurous should head down to the bottom of Via Krupp, where huge flat stones lie along the shore.

View over the bay, Capri

5 Ischia
To gain access to any beach here – at least the good parts – you will need to pay, but for around €15 to €20 per day, you receive the use of a sunbed and an umbrella. There are plenty of beaches to choose from, including sandy stretches in Forio and Ischia Porto (see p101). More out-of-the-way options include San Montano and Sorgeto.

Sant'Angello, Ischia

Marina Grande beach, Amalfi

6 Amalfi

Lined with colourful umbrellas (see p104), the Marina Grande beach has a free area popular with locals. Or take a short boat ride to the rocky Santa Croce beach.

7 Positano

Again, at this fashionable, busy resort, payment is necessary for a sunbed and umbrella (see p104). For something more independent take the path to the west, around the cliff, to the beach at Fornillo – it's smaller and rockier but more relaxed.

8 Marina di Praia

This small cove, just beyond Positano (see p107), has a bit of beach you can generally call your own, as few tourists stop here. However you will share the cove with local fishing boats, a couple of bar-restaurants, a diving centre and the coast's premier disco, Africana.

9 Marina di Furore
MAP E5

A very precipitous path goes straight down to this dramatic, tiny beach set between the cliffs. A few fishermen's homes cluster here, with their boats neatly moored along one side, and there's a bar-restaurant.

10 Erchie and Cetara
MAP F4

The beach at Erchie is a small cove graced by a watchtower, fishing boats and a few houses. At Cetara, bathers share the narrow rocky strip with boats, but it's good for a dip.

TOP 10 SPAS

1 Terme di Agnano, Naples
MAP J2 ▪ Via Agnano Astroni 24
A spa since ancient times. Mud-baths and mineral waters.

2 Giardini Poseidon, Ischia
MAP B4 ▪ Via Mazzella
Saunas, Jacuzzis, pools and treatments.

3 Negombo, Ischia
MAP A4 ▪ Via Baia di S Montano, Lacco Ameno
Surrounded by beautiful gardens with volcanic springs.

4 Parco Termale Aphrodite Apollon, Ischia
MAP A4 ▪ Via Petrelle, Sant'Angelo
Pools, saunas and massage.

5 Terme Belliazzi, Ischia
MAP A4 ▪ Piazza Bagni 134, Casamicciola
Mud treatments and massage.

6 Terme di Cava Scura, Ischia
MAP A4 ▪ Via Cava Scura, Serrara Fontana
Built into the cliffs, with a cave sauna and baths in sulphurous water.

7 Terme della Regina Isabella, Ischia
MAP A4 ▪ Piazza Sta Restituta, Lacco Ameno
Luxury massage and treatments.

8 Capri Palace Hotel
Anacapri's top hotel also has a spa and beauty treatment centre (see p129).

9 Hotel Capo La Gala, Vico Equense
MAP D4 ▪ Via Luigi Serio 8
Next to Spa Scrajo; enjoy the mineral water swimming pool.

10 Terme di Stabia, Castellammare di Stabia
MAP E4 ▪ Viale delle Terme 3–5
Mud, mineral waters and massage.

Parco Termale Aphrodite Apollon

🔟 Walks

Wonderful landscape for walking on Capri

1 Decumano Maggiore
MAP P2

In Roman times this street, now known as Via dei Tribunali, was the main east–west artery of the city. Decumano Maggiore constitutes the heart of the old quarter and is replete with unmissable sights, as well as intriguing shops and bars and cafés to while away the hours.

2 Royal Naples
MAP P4

For regal edifices and elegant cafés and shops, this choice part of town is pedestrian-friendly. A good place to start is the Fontana del Nettuno on Via Medina (see p50) and then head towards the sea and west. This arc takes in Castel Nuovo, Teatro San Carlo and Galleria Umberto I.

Castel Nuovo, Naples

3 Capri

Once you break away from the smart shops and hotels, this island (see pp34–5) is all about nature walks: up to Villa Jovis, down to the Arco Naturale, along the Sentiero dei Fortini to the Blue Grotto – the possibilities are numerous.

4 Spaccanapoli

The colloquial name of this ancient street (see pp76–85) means "Splits Naples", which is exactly what it does, cutting the oldest part of the city right down the middle. Beginning at the western end in Piazza del Gesù Nuovo, a straight line takes you past some of the city's finest monuments, and there are shops, bars, cafés and pizzerias.

5 Lungomare
MAP N6

Beginning at the public gardens next to the Palazzo Reale, take the seaside road around the Santa Lucia quarter and past some of Naples' loveliest areas, including the island of Castel dell'Ovo and the green splendour of the Villa Comunale.

6 Via Toledo
MAP N3

From the royal quarter Via Toledo begins elegantly, but soon the

Quartieri Spagnoli (Spanish Quarters) come up along the western flank – a warren of narrow, dark streets that hide some of the city's best-kept secrets. However, continuing on, you'll pass Piazza Dante and finally come to the Museo Archeologico.

Sorrentine Peninsula
MAP D5

If you take the *funivia* (cable car) from Castellammare di Stabia up to Monte Faito there are startling views from the top, as well as the beginning of many nature trails, some of which eventually lead as far as Positano.

8 The Amalfi Coast

Hiking points can be reached above Positano and between Ravello and Amalfi-Atrani. Most of these paths are erstwhile goat trails – the most famous is the *Sentieri degli Dei* (Path of the Gods) – while some have been built up as stone stairways *(see p103)*; all offer incomparable views.

Walking the rim of Mount Vesuvius

9 Vesuvius

A walk along the rim of this vast crater *(see p95)* is an experience of a lifetime. Some 20,000 visitors a year trek to the top to peer into the steaming depths 200 m (700 ft) below. The steep hike up takes about 30 minutes and it's at its best in late spring, when flowers are most vibrant.

10 Ischia

The walks and hikes on this island *(see p101)* are plentiful. A memorable trek is up Monte Epomeo from Forio, through Fontana, taking about 40 minutes.

TOP 10 DRIVES

Vietri from above

1 Positano to Vietri
MAP E5
A single road "of 1,000 turns" winds along this spectacular coast.

2 Sorrento to Positano
MAP D5
Follow the signs to Santa Agata sui Due Golfi and then Colli di Fontanelle to get your first glimpse of Positano.

3 Amalfi to Ravello
MAP E5
Leave the coast road and climb up and up for a vista unlike any other.

4 Over the Monti Lattari
MAP E5
Wind through mountain meadows before the descent to the Amalfi Coast.

5 Around Ischia
MAP B4
A fairly good road rings the island.

6 Naples to Sorrento
MAP E4
Cut off the tollway to Castellammare di Stabia and take the picturesque road.

7 Marina Grande to Anacapri, Capri
MAP S1
The cliff road is best experienced in the island's classic open-top taxis.

8 The Phlegrean Fields
MAP J2
Hug the coastline from Posillipo to Pozzuoli and take local roads to Agnano Terme and La Solfatara.

9 Cumae
MAP B3
Begin at Lago d'Averno and pass under the Arco Felice to arrive at Cumae.

10 Naples to Paestum
MAP H6
Take the A3, then switch to the N19, direction Battipaglia. Take the right fork for Paestum, the N18 south.

🔟 Off the Beaten Track

1 Green Grotto, Capri
MAP T2

On the other side of the island from its far more famous sibling, the Blue Grotto (see p35), this smaller cave glows emerald green once you duck inside. The best way to get here is to rent a kayak at Punta Carena and then make your way past Marina Piccola towards the Faraglioni rocks.

Green Grotto entrance, Capri

2 Napoli Sotterranea
MAP P2 ▪ Piazza S Gaetano 68 ▪ 081 29 69 44 ▪ Guided tours in English: 10am, noon, 2pm, 4pm & 6pm ▪ Adm ▪ www.napolisotterranea.org

This tour's entrance is next to San Paolo Maggiore (see p80) and takes you into a world of excavations that date back to the 4th century BC (bring a jacket as it can be cool). The digging began when the Greeks quarried large tufa blocks to build the city of Neapolis. Caves were also dug here to be used as tombs. Centuries later the Romans turned this underground area into aqueducts and cisterns, which were in use until the cholera epidemic of 1884.

3 San Gaudioso Catacombs
MAP K2 ▪ Basilica of Sta Maria della Sanità, Via della Sanità 124 ▪ Guided tours: every hour between 10am & 1pm ▪ Adm ▪ www. catacombedinapoli.it

This labyrinth of underground tunnels was built by the Romans for use as cisterns. It evolved into catacombs in the 5th century, when St Gaudiosus, a North African bishop and hermit, was interred here. Visitors can see the remains of fresco and mosaic decorations.

4 Spiaggia di Fornillo, Positano
Few know that there's an alternative to the main beach at Positano, with rows of sunbeds and umbrellas. To get to Fornillo, head west on the path past the Lo Guarracino restaurant, around the cliff. It's a rocky beach (see p59), overlooked by two towers, but there's a café-restaurant and facilities.

5 Cimitero delle Fontanelle
MAP K1 ▪ Via delle Fontanelle 80 ▪ 081 192 569 64 ▪ 10 am–5pm daily

Once a Roman quarry for tufa blocks, this cavern became a depository for the city's dead during the cholera epidemic of 1884. Graves and tombs were emptied all over Naples and the skulls stacked here – some 40,000 in all, with the addition of still more during the cholera outbreak of 1974.

Skulls, Cimitero delle Fontanelle

Colourful galleries, at MADRE

6 MADRE
MAP P1 ▪ Via Settembrini 79 ▪ 081 197 372 54 ▪ Open 10am–7:30pm Wed–Mon (to 8pm Sun) ▪ Adm ▪ www.madrenapoli.it

This museum of contemporary art is housed in a 14th-century church. Exhibitions from the 1940s onwards contrast with the surrounding history of Naples. Permanent exhibitions include the Historical Collection.

7 Sibyl's Grotto, Cumae
This grotto is believed to be a Roman military structure by some and a mythological one by others. The wedge-shaped walls, coupled with the lighting, create a hypnotic effect.

8 Tomb of Virgil and Crypta Neapolitana
MAP K2 ▪ Salita della Grotta 20, Mergellina ▪ Open 9am–5pm Wed–Mon (winter: 10am–2:50pm)

What is known as Virgil's tomb is a Roman burial vault from the Augustan age. It is a typical dovecote style of burial, with niches for urns containing the ashes of the deceased. Next to the tomb are a tufa quarry and a *crypta* (tunnel), built as an underground road in the 1st century BC.

9 Parco Sommerso, Baia
MAP B3 ▪ Glass-bottom boat tours or land tours: call 349 497 41 83 or visit www.baiasommersa.it; diving and snorkelling tours: call 081 853 15 63

Most of the ancient city of Baia now lies underwater *(see p112)*. Just below the surface of the water are remnants of the port and parts of various villas and temples.

10 San Gennaro Catacombs
MAP K1 ▪ Via Capodimonte 13 ▪ Guided tours: every hour between 10am & 7pm Mon–Sat, between 10am & 1pm Sun and public hols ▪ Adm

Burials here date back to the 2nd century. In the 5th century, the body of San Gennaro, Naples' patron saint, was brought here, and the place became an important pilgrimage site. Frescoes and mosaics on the two levels of this vast layout attest to its importance.

🔟 Children's Attractions

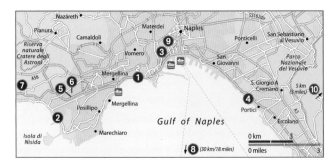

1 Villa Comunale

This urban park in central Naples *(see p88)* has a playground designed for little ones and there are always plenty of families enjoying the gardens and walkways. The biggest attraction here may be the Stazione Zoologica (Zoological Institute), the oldest aquarium in Europe, featuring sea life from the Bay of Naples.

2 Pietrarsa Railway Museum

MAP D3 ▪ Via Pietrarsa, Portici ▪ 081 567 23 02 ▪ Open 2–8pm Thu, 9am–4:30pm Fri, 9:30am–7:30pm Sat & Sun ▪ www.museopietrarsa.it ▪ Adm

Italy's first railway was inaugurated by King Ferdinand II in 1839 and 150 years later the railway workshop was

Exhibit, Pietrarsa Railway Museum

opened as a museum. It is the largest of its kind in Europe and has impressive displays, such as a reconstruction of the first royal train and a line-up of the later, lavishly gilded carriages.

3 Centro Musei delle Scienze Naturali

MAP P3 ▪ Via Mezzocannone 8 & Largo S Marcellino 10 ▪ 081 253 75 87 ▪ Open 9am–1:30pm Mon–Fri (also open 2:15–4:30pm Mon & Thu) ▪ Adm ▪ www.cmsnf.it

The Università di Napoli Federico II houses five museums in one building with sections on Physics, Mineralogy, Anthropology, Zoology and Palaeontology, the latter with fascinating dinosaur exhibits.

4 Science City

A hands-on "experimentorium", *(see p114)* with something for everyone. Included in the exhibits are up-to-date computer gizmos that seem to transcend language barriers, and a planetarium (booking ahead is compulsory and incurs an extra fee).

5 Edenlandia

MAP J2 ▪ Viale Kennedy, Fuorigrotta ▪ 081 239 40 90 ▪ Open Jul: 5pm–midnight Tue–Sun (to 10:30pm Sun); Aug: 10:30pm–midnight daily; hours vary rest of the year (phone or check website for details) ▪ Adm ▪ edenlandiapark.it

This ageing amusement park is a favourite of the locals. Rides include a Big Dipper, a Ghost Train, a Canoe Flume and Bumper Cars, as well as several more hightech options. An old-fashioned choice that never fails to delight is Le Nuvole, a theatre group that features puppets and mime.

⑥ Zoo di Napoli
MAP C3 ▪ Via J F Kennedy 76 ▪ 081 193 631 54 ▪ Open Apr–Oct: 9:30am–7pm; Nov–Mar: 9:30am–5pm ▪ Adm ▪ www.lozoodinapoli.com

Home to more than 400 animals, the zoo allows visitors to pet them up close and, in some cases, get in the pens with the zookeepers. Educational activities are also organized for kids.

⑦ Solfatara
A geothermal playground that will fascinate budding geologists, this congealed lava cap plugging up a dormant volcano is an expanse of hissing, bubbling terrain *(see p114)*. There's even a camp site with restaurant – you soon get used to the sulphur smell.

⑧ Vesuvius
No child will ever forget a trip up this killer volcano *(see p95)* and a peek over the rim into the steaming abyss below. It's a fairly short, steep walk – only about half an hour – and the thrill will stay with them for years.

Marina Piccola Beach, Capri

⑨ Ospedale delle Bambole
MAP P2 ▪ Via S Biagio dei Librai 81 ▪ 081 20 30 67 ▪ Open 10am–4:30pm Mon–Fri (to 3pm Sat) ▪ www.ospedaledellebambole.it

Children are captivated by the Doll Hospital, both for the concept as well as for the array of dolls that are here waiting to be "cured". Adults, too, will find this unique workshop fascinating. There is also a shop, so your child won't necessarily have to say goodbye to a new-found friend.

Dolls, Ospedale delle Bambole

⑩ Marina Piccola Beach, Capri
One of the most child-friendly beaches in the area *(see p34)*: the water is tranquil and the bathing areas well protected. For all the toys and gear you might need, there are shops handy, and a choice of places to eat. Changing rooms and sunbeds are available.

🔟 Neapolitan Dishes

1 Contorni

The fertility of the land around Naples is most evident when you taste the produce it brings forth. For *contorni* (side dishes), peppers, artichokes, aubergine (eggplant), capers, mushrooms and green beans are offered steamed or sautéed. Expect the freshness to have been retained fully, cooked with a touch of garlic, tomato or lemon, and herbs.

Insalata caprese

2 Primo

This course usually means pasta or rice, but *minestre* and *zuppe* (soups) also appear in this category. Great *primi* to look out for are *spaghetti alle vongole veraci* (with clams), *pasta e fagioli* (with beans), *fettucine alla puttanesca* (egg noodles with tomato, capers, black olives and red pepper) and *risotto alla pescatora* (rice with seafood).

the wonderful salads (*insalata*) here, there are two famous cold dishes from the area. The *insalata caprese* is the essence of simplicity, relying on quality *mozzarella di bufala*, tomatoes and aromatic basil. *Caponata* may include marinated aubergine (eggplant), artichoke hearts and capers, with bread to soak up the flavours.

5 Pizza

Perhaps it's the water, or the quality of the flour or yeast used, but Neapolitan pizza is inimitable. It's spongy, chewy, succulent and melts in your mouth, while the toppings are flavourful and aromatic. Purists insist that it was invented here centuries ago and that the only true pizza is the *margherita* – tomato, basil and mozzarella cheese, with olive oil.

Spaghetti alle vongole veraci

3 Secondo

Main course dishes come in two varieties, *mare* (sea) and *terra* (land). Fresh seafood, especially *vongole* (clams) and *cozze* (mussels), are popular along the coast. Meat dishes are varied and include *polpette* (meatballs), *salsiccia* (sausage) with broccoli and *coniglio* (rabbit), a speciality on Ischia.

4 Insalata

Besides the host of fresh leaves and cherry tomatoes that end up in

Neapolitan pizza

6 Fish and Seafood

This category is the area's strong point. *Calamari* (squid) are a favourite, as are *cozze* (mussels) in a variety of presentations. *Seppie* (cuttlefish) and *polipo* (octopus) are popular, too, stewed, fried or steamed. *Pesce all'acqua pazza* (fish in "crazy water") is a treat – fresh fish stewed in water with tomatoes, garlic and chillies.

7 Formaggi

Mozzarella di bufala is the signature cheese from the area. The milk of the buffalo has a tangy quality and the cheese a unique smoothness. The smoked version is *provola*.

Antipasti of olives and cured meats

8 Antipasti

The first course may be marinated fish or seafood, a selection of olives and cured meats, *bruschetta* (toasted bread) with various toppings or *prosciutto* (ham) with figs or melon, depending on the season.

9 Dolci

Many Neapolitan desserts are inspired by their Sicilian cousins, notably *delizie*, a cream-filled cake, and *pannacotta* (cooked cream), perhaps topped with fresh fruit. In season, the melon, figs and wild strawberries are unforgettable.

10 Pastries

A *sfogliatella* (pastry filled with ricotta cheese) is a sublime way to start the day, accompanied by a cup of coffee. Other treats include *babà* (cake soaked in rum and honey) and *zeppole* (pastry filled with custard and topped with wild cherries).

TOP 10 LOCAL DRINKS

1 White Wine
Campania wines are of a very high quality. Falanghina, Greco di Tufo and Lacryma Christi are reliable names.

2 Red Wine
Full-bodied reds come from the local Aglianico grape.

3 Liqueurs
The most famous of these is the lemon liqueur *limoncello*, which delivers quite a kick.

4 Beer
All major brands are available, but a local Italian favourite is Peroni. If you want draught, ask for *alla spina*.

5 Mineral Water
Italians enjoy a huge array of mineral waters. A great choice is Ferrarelle – or for something lighter, Uliveto.

6 Digestivi
Many restaurants produce their own digestive concoctions – pure alcohol with a soothing mixture of spices and flavourings.

7 Coffee
Neapolitan-style coffee traditionally comes already sweetened, and it is generally very concentrated.

8 Soft Drinks
The usual range of choices is available, but an interesting Italian cola-type drink is Chinotto.

9 Infusioni
Camomilla (camomile) is considered to be a relaxant, while other herbal teas on offer include *menta* (peppermint) and *tiglio* (lime-tree).

10 Spremute
Most bars are set up, in summer, to turn out freshly squeezed orange juice and a local version of lemonade.

Limoncello **for sale**

🔟 Neapolitan Souvenirs

1 Coral and Cameos

The tradition of miniature carvings in stone is an ancient one – the Romans (and their Renaissance imitators) used precious and semi-precious stones, from agate to emerald, as well as layered glass. Today the tradition *(see p96)* primarily focuses on gems from the sea. Coral is prized for its rich colours and soft texture, while shells are fashioned into delicate cameos.

2 Handmade Paper and Cards

Amalfi was once home to a thriving paper industry, which features at the Museo della Carta *(see p47)*. The tradition is still on display in local shops selling handmade paper, stationery and beautiful journals.

A traditional ceramic plate

3 Antiques

The area remains one of the great sources for antiques; especially plentiful are Baroque and Rococo furniture, as well as Empire pieces. Antique ceramics, too, are a good buy, notably handpainted tiles.

4 Copies of Antiquities

Believe it or not, souvenir stalls outside archaeological sites – notably Pompeii – can be good sources of creditable copies of famous Roman sculptures, but you'll need to pick through the junk and be prepared to bargain.

5 Ceramics

Ceramics – both copies of traditional designs and original creations – are notable in Capri, Ravello and Vietri.

6 Gouaches

Gouache is a watercolour paint applied to heavy paper that gives a very soft yet vibrant look to the surface of a painting. In the 19th century gouache land-scapes of Naples, its bay and Vesuvius were produced in great numbers and many are still available at reasonable prices. These were the postcard souvenirs for Grand Tour visitors, and to the modern eye they evoke a sense of idyllic charm. There are also prints of the more famous scenes.

7 Gold

Italian artisans have been famed for centuries for their gold-work. Neapolitan artists have inherited these traditions since ancient times and local jewel-lery shops attest to the beauty of their crea-tions. All gold used is at least 18 carat and prices are comparable with those in other coun-tries, while the quality is higher. Head for Borgo degli Orefici, the Goldsmiths' District.

Shopping for antiques in Naples

Figures depicting a nativity scene

8 Nativity Figures

For centuries Naples has been internationally noted for its production of figures for nativity scenes, many produced by the very best sculptors, especially in the 18th century, and reproduced to this day by skilled artisans whose *botteghe* (workshops) line the streets of the old town. A popular secular figure, done in a variety of media, including terracotta, *papier mâché*, wood, or a combination of materials, is Pulcinella (see p44). There are also delightful puppets, dolls and masks.

Cobbler crafting sandals, Capri

9 Handmade Sandals, Capri

There are a number of cobblers on the island of Capri (see p106) who will make made-to-measure sandals within a matter of hours.

10 Intarsio, Sorrento

Renowned for centuries for its gorgeous *intarsio* (marquetry), Sorrento continues the tradition to this day, and some of the pieces are true works of art.

TOP 10 MARKETS

A shop at La Pignasecca

1 La Pignasecca, Naples
MAP M3 ▪ Via Pignasecca
▪ 8am–1pm daily
One of Naples' oldest markets and as cheap as it gets.

2 Poggioreale
MAP L1 ▪ Via M di Caramanico
▪ 6am–2pm Fri–Sun
Naples' largest market has piles of everything, especially shoes.

3 San Pasquale, Naples
MAP K6 ▪ Via S Pasquale
▪ 8am–2pm Mon, Wed, Fri–Sat
Spices, fish, clothing and jewellery.

4 Fiera Antiquaria Napoletana, Naples
MAP K6 ▪ Villa Comunale
▪ 7am–2pm 3rd Sat & Sun of month
As much junk as antiques, but great fun.

5 Atignano, Naples
MAP K2 ▪ Via Luca Giordano, Vomero ▪ 7am–2pm Mon–Sat
Household items.

6 Fuorigrotta, Naples
MAP J2 ▪ Via Metastasio ▪ 8am–1pm daily
Food, household items and more.

7 Porta Nolana, Naples
MAP R2 ▪ Piazza Nolana ▪ 8am–2pm daily
Chaotic fish market.

8 Resina, Ercolano
MAP L2 ▪ Via Pugliano
▪ 8am–1pm daily
Roman "antiques".

9 La Fiera di Icaro, Naples
MAP J1 ▪ Via Antica di Chiaiano, 1A
▪ 7am–1:30pm Sat
As much trash as treasure.

10 Posillipo
MAP K1 ▪ Viale Virgilio
▪ 9am–2pm Thu
Clothing, shoes and bags.

Naples and the Amalfi Coast for Free

Views over Marina Grande, Sorrento, with Mount Vesuvius on the horizon

1 Marina Grande, Sorrento
MAP D5

Sorrento's Marina Grande harbour is one of the most charming spots in town, with its rows of colourful fishing boats bobbing in the water and multihued homes that were once home to fisherman.

2 Castel dell'Ovo, Naples
With a scenic setting on an islet in the Bay of Naples, entrance to the Castel dell'Ovo is free, and everyone in the family will enjoy exploring the castle while taking in the outstanding views *(see p88)*.

3 Villa Romana, Minori
For a glimpse of ancient Roman history on the Amalfi Coast, visit the ruins of a wealthy family villa that have been excavated in the heart of Minori *(see p105)*.

4 Spaccanapoli, Naples
MAP P2

This narrow main street cuts straight through the historic centre of the city and captures the vibrant atmosphere that is Naples. Enjoy a stroll past fine monuments while visiting free churches like the Gesù Nuovo and San Domenico Maggiore *(see p80)*. Today the street is officially named Via Benedetto Croce and moving east it changes to Via S Biagio dei Librai *(see pp76–85)*.

5 Via Positanesi d'America, Positano
MAP E5

Connecting Positano's Spiaggia Grande with the more secluded Spiaggia di Fornillo *(see p62)*, this cliff-hugging pathway is one of the prettiest walks on the Amalfi Coast.

6 Galleria Umberto I, Naples
The soaring glass roof, Neo-Renaissance designs and marble floors of the Galleria Umberto I make this 19th-century shopping gallery worth seeing for its architecture alone *(see p88)*.

Galleria Umberto I, Naples

Auditorium Oscar Niemeyer, Ravello

MAP E4 ▪ Via della Repubblica 12
▪ 089 85 83 60

This rare example of modern design is named after its creator, Brazilian architect Oscar Niemeyer. While only open for events, its large terrace offers the same outstanding views you would pay to see at the Villa Rufolo nearby.

8 Arco Naturale, Capri
MAP C5

While the price tag of many of Capri's sights can shock, the natural beauty is as easy on the eyes as it is on the budget. For a beautiful walk, follow signs from the Piazzetta in Capri Town to the Arco Naturale *(see p34)*.

Arco Naturale, Capri

9 Duomo, Naples

While there is an admission charge to visit the cathedral's museum and archaeological area, it is free to visit the soaring nave of the Duomo and the dazzling Cappella di San Gennaro *(see pp16–17)*.

10 Villa Comunale, Naples

This 18th-century urban park was designed by Luigi Vanvitelli, the mastermind behind the grandiose Reggia di Caserta. With playgrounds, classic statues and beautiful views, it's a family friendly spot to while away an afternoon *(see p88)*.

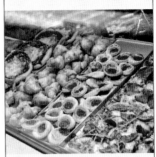

TOP 10 MONEY-SAVING TIPS

Street food, Naples

1 Naples is famous for its street food, which is a delicious way to save money and experience local specialities.

2 Visit Naples from October to April (but not Christmas) when low-season rates and discounts will delight the budget-minded traveller.

3 Note that many hotels and restaurants on the Amalfi Coast and Capri close during the winter, however, rates are often lower for the shoulder season October to November and February to March.

4 Most beaches have a *spiaggia libera* area where you do not have to pay to access the beach.

5 Parking can be exceedingly expensive and limited on the Amalfi Coast, so traveling by public transport is recommended.

6 Save money on visits to many sights in Naples and throughout the region with the Campania Artecard, see www.campaniartecard.it.

7 Take the Circumvesuviana train for an inexpensive way to travel between Naples, Sorrento, Pompeii and Herculaneum.

8 The ferry between Positano and Amalfi is an affordable way to see the beauty of the Amalfi Coast from the sea.

9 Alibus runs a cheap shuttle from the Naples airport to the Napoli Centrale train station and port.

10 Many museums and archaeological sites offer a free open day during the week or month.

Religious Celebrations

La Befana, festival of the Epiphany

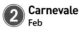 La Befana
6 Jan

In Italy the festival of the Epiphany is personified by La Befana, a witch-like hag flying in on a broom who delivers gifts to good children and puts "lumps of coal" (actually sweets) in the shoes of naughty ones.

2 Carnevale
Feb

Pulcinella (see p50) is lord of this blow-out in Naples, just before the austerities of Lent begin. Lasagne is the dish to indulge in, and masks and partying are very much a part of this age-old celebration. Kids get the chance to choose their fantasy persona and parade around in their finery.

 Pucinella figurines, Carnevale

3 Pasqua
Mar or Apr

In Italy, Pasqua (Easter Sunday) and Pasquetta (Easter Monday) are both important, as is the week leading up to them in some towns. Good Friday processions are held around the Naples area, with an especially rich one on the island of Procida. Pasquetta is traditionally a day for outings – picnics being a top choice to celebrate the advent of spring. Near Sant'Anastasia, 15 km (9 miles) east of Naples, a festival is held at the sanctuary of the Madonna dell'Arco.

San Gennaro
The Saturday before the first Sunday in May is the first of a thrice-yearly event. During this celebration, the blood of Naples' patron saint – who has seen the city through earthquakes, volcanic eruptions and football championships – flows again. The miracle is received with a hysteria seldom seen in this day and age – a manifestation of age-old faith that involves flower-bedecked processions of the saint's effigy through the old quarter.

5 San Giovanni
24 Jun

The feast day of St John the Baptist also sometimes sees his blood boil – a phial of it is ensconced in the church of San Gregorio Armeno (see p80). Otherwise, the saint is traditionally remembered in charmingly pagan ways, linked to the summer solstice: night bathing, magicians and the gathering of walnuts to make nocino, a liqueur prepared for late autumn.

6 Santa Maria del Carmine
15–17 Jul

Every summer, Naples' tallest bell tower is "burned" in commemoration of a legend (see p80) that recounts how an icon kept here, the Madonna Bruna, saved it from being destroyed by fire. An array of fireworks are dramatically set off at the climax of the festivities.

Ferragosto
15 Aug

The Assumption of the Virgin Mary marks the height of the summer season, when most shops and restaurants close in the city (although not on the coast). Pozzuoli stages a contest of climbing a greased pole, while Positano re-enacts a landing of Saracen corsairs.

 Madonna di Piedigrotta
Sep

Once a fancy affair, today the event involves a song competition and theatrical events, plus fireworks and street parties. It all centres on a 14th-century sculpture of the Madonna and Child.

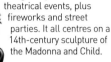 **L'Immacolata**
8 Dec

Celebrating the Immaculate Conception, this festival opens the Christmas season; nativity scenes and decorations go up and the Guglia dell' Immacolata *(see p78)* in Piazza del Gesù becomes the focal point of activity.

Guglia dell'Immacolata

Natale
24–25 Dec

At Christmas the streets around San Gregorio Armeno *(see p80)* are full of shoppers looking for items to complete their nativity scenes, and concerts take place in the churches.

Christmas nativity scene

TOP 10 SECULAR FESTIVALS

Festival delle Ville Vesuviane

1 Culture Week
Apr
For one week publicly owned museums, historic and archaeological sites are free.

2 Maggio dei Monumenti
May
Churches and buildings usually closed to the public open for one week.

3 Estate a Napoli
Summer in Naples includes outdoor films, theatre and music.

4 The Regatta of the Maritime Republics, Amalfi
Jun
Every four years Amalfi hosts a boat race against Venice, Pisa and Genoa.

5 Pizza Village, Naples
Jun
A celebration of the city's famous dish, as pizza-makers spin their dough.

6 Concerti al Tramonto, Villa San Michele, Anacapri
Jun–Aug
This genteel villa is the venue for sunset classical concerts *(see p35)*.

7 Ravello Festival
Jun–Sep
A rich calendar of music, theatre and dance in evocative settings *(see p37)*.

8 Neapolis Festival
Jul
Southern Italy's largest rockfest invades the area of Bagnoli.

9 Festival delle Ville Vesuviane
Jul
The aristocratic villas along this coast play host to classical concerts *(see p96)*.

10 Capodanno, Naples
31 Dec
New Year's Eve involves merrymaking and fireworks over Castel dell'Ovo.

Naples and the Amalfi Coast Area by Area

Procida, crammed with ancient
buildings painted in lively colours

TOP10 Spaccanapoli to Capodimonte

The ancient heart of the city is celebrated for its striking juxtaposition of chaos and consummate artistry, but most of all for the sheer, boundless energy of the Neapolitan spirit. In many ways, it is an atavistic realm, ruled by its past, including innumerable disasters, but it is also a city with an awareness of its abiding glories, and Old Naples has opened anew to the world. Its narrow streets are much safer and cleaner than before and its erstwhile dilapidated, shut-away treasures are now restored and far better organized, without losing any of their uniquely vibrant feeling. Spaccanapoli is the colloquial name for the long, narrow street that runs from Via Duomo to Via Monteoliveto and is the remnant of an ancient Greco-Roman thoroughfare.

Statue, Museo Archeologico

SPACCANAPOLI TO CAPODIMONTE

1 Top 10 Sights
see pp77–9

1 Restaurants
see p85

1 Traditional Shops
see p81

1 Old Naples by Night
see p82

1 Pizzerie
see p84

1 Churches
see p80

1 Cafés, Gelaterie and Pasticcerie see p83

0 metres   200
0 yards   200

Impressive interior of the Duomo

1 Duomo

Although its position in the present-day street-plan seems to be an afterthought and the perfunctory Neo-Gothic façade (see pp16–17) is less than inspiring, inside Naples' cathedral is a fascinating cornucopia of history, art and culture. There are ancient remains of the Greek and Roman cities to explore, including some beautiful paleo-Christian mosaics in the baptistry, and splendid art abounds in the main church and its chapels, including the huge work dedicated to the city's patron saint, Gennaro (Januarius).

2 Museo Archeologico

One of the world's most important museums of ancient art houses some of the most famous statues from the Greco-Roman past, such as the Callipygean Venus that set standards of physical beauty that have endured through the ages (see pp18–21). Other monumental marble works include the Farnese Hercules, but the collections also feature bronzes, mosaics, frescoes, carved semi-precious stone, glassware, Greek vases and Egyptian mummies.

Cloister tiles detail, Santa Chiara

3 Santa Chiara

MAP N3 ▪ Via Santa Chiara 49c ▪ 081 551 66 73 ▪ Open 7:30am–1pm, 4:30–8pm daily (church); 9:30am–6pm Mon–Sat, 10am–2:30pm Sun & public hols (museum & cloister) ▪ Adm (church free) ▪ monasterodi santachiara.it

The façade of this structure (see p44), rebuilt after World War II, is like a huge cliff of buff-coloured tufa, relieved only by its portico and giant rose window. Only the base of its 14th-century bell tower is original. Inside the decor has been returned to its Gothic origins, since all the Baroque embellishment was destroyed in wartime bombings. The tomb of Robert of Anjou is the largest funerary monument of medieval Italy, and behind this is the delightful tiled cloister.

4 Museo di Capodimonte

This royal palace *(see pp22–3)* is home to important works by some of the greatest masters, including Botticelli, Filippino Lippi, Mantegna, Bellini, Fra' Bartolomeo, Michelangelo, Raphael, Titian, Rembrandt and Dürer, as well as by every great painter working in Naples during the 17th and 18th centuries, including Caravaggio and Vivarini.

Virgin with Child Enthroned (1465) by Bartolomeo Vivarini, Capodimonte

5 Palazzo dello Spagnolo

MAP P1 ▪ Via Vergini 19

Dating from 1728, this palace offers a fine example of a well-known Neapolitan architectural element, the staircase *"ad ali di falco"* (with falcon wings). Separating two courtyards, the external stairway consists of double flights of steps with tiers of archways, a feature that became the trademark of its designer, Ferdinando Sanfelice. Stucco designs can be seen throughout; particular attention to detail is evident above doorways.

6 Santi Apostoli

MAP P1 ▪ Largo Santi Apostoli 9 ▪ Open 9am–noon, 5–8pm Mon–Sat, 9am–1pm Sun

The original church on this site is believed to have been built in the 5th century over a Roman temple to Mercury. It was rebuilt in the 17th century, with decoration added over the next 100 years. As such it provides a complete treasury of 17th- and 18th-century art, not just by

---

THE THREE GUGLIE

The area's three *guglie* ("needles" or "spires") imitate the original towering contraptions built in the 1600s and 1700s to celebrate feast days. The first stone *guglia* was raised to San Gennaro, when the saint supposedly saved Naples from Vesuvius's fury in 1631. Next came one dedicated to San Domenico, as thanks for the end of the 1656 plague. The last adorns Piazza del Gesù, dedicated to the Immaculate Virgin.

Neapolitan artists but by some of the greatest masters of the day. Most famous is the fresco cycle by Lanfranco, with a marvellous trompe-l'oeil architectural setting by Codazzi. Another highlight is the altar that was designed by Borromini.

7 San Giovanni a Carbonara

MAP Q1 ▪ Via Carbonara 5 ▪ Open 9am–6pm Mon–Sat, 8am–2pm Sun

This 14th-century church has no façade of its own but is reached by a double staircase through a courtyard to the left of the Chapel of Santa Monica. Inside is a circular chapel with 15th-century frescoes and bas-reliefs by Spanish masters Bartolomé Ordoñez and Diego de Siloe.

Chapel, San Giovanni a Carbonara

8 Orto Botanico

MAP K1 ▪ Via Floria 223 ▪ 081 253 39 37 ▪ Open 9am–2pm Mon, Wed & Fri, 9am–4pm Tue & Thu by appt only ▪ Guided tours Mar–May ▪ www.ortobotanico.unina.it

Created in 1807, this botanical garden is one of Italy's most important. Given Naples' climate, it has been possible to cultivate examples of nearly all of the world's plants and flowers here. Historic structures include the Neo-Classical Serra Temperata, built in 1807 and the double stairway entrance to the grounds.

Cactus display, Orto Botanico

9 Sansevero Chapel

MAP P2 ▪ Via Francesco de Sanctis 19 ▪ 081 552 49 36 ▪ Open 9am–7pm Wed–Mon ▪ Adm ▪ www.museosansevero.it

Few spaces are decorated with such unity as this family chapel, designed by the eccentric 18th-century prince Raimondo di Sangro. Full of allegorical symbolism, the statuary are among Naples' most famous, particularly the "veiled" figures of Christ and Modesty. Don't miss the Anatomical Machines.

10 Piazza Bellini

MAP N2

One of the most appealing places in Naples is lined with cafés, bookshops and palaces. Of particular note is the monastery of Sant'Antonio a Port'Alba, (see p46) incorporating 15th-century Palazzo Conca. At the centre of the piazza, in addition to a statue of the eponymous composer, is an archaeological excavation, revealing 5th-century BC Greek walls of large tufa blocks.

A MORNING AT OLD NAPLES' CHURCHES

▶ Begin your tour of Naples' two oldest main streets at Piazza del Gesù Nuovo, where you can admire the Guglia dell'Immacolata and the rusticated façade of the **Gesù Nuovo** (see p80). Further along, enter **Santa Chiara** (see p77) to take in the medieval tombs and then around the back to see the famous tiled cloister.

Continuing on, stop for a drink at one of the cafés in Piazza San Domenico, where you will note that the Guglia di San Domenico has mermaids sculpted on its base. Across the street, stop in at the church of **Sant'Angelo a Nilo** (see p80) to see its Donatello bas-relief, and at the next corner, look for the ancient statue of the god of the Nile, known familiarly as "The Body of Naples". Follow the street all the way to Via Duomo, pausing at the shops of all kinds along the way.

Next, visit the culturally amazing **Duomo** (see pp16–17), and then go behind it to see the earliest *guglia*, topped by a statue of San Gennaro, and Caravaggio's revolutionary painting *The Acts of Mercy* in the **Pio Monte della Misericordia** (see p45). Double back along Via dei Tribunali, where you can visit more fascinating churches, including **San Gregorio Armeno** (see p80) and **Santa Maria delle Anime del Purgatorio ad Arco** (see p80).

Finally, head for **Piazza Bellini**, where you can watch the world go by and have a drink or a full meal at one of the friendly cafés.

See map on pp76–7

Churches

Detail of the elaborate ceiling, San Lorenzo Maggiore

1 San Lorenzo Maggiore
MAP P2 ■ Via dei Tribunali 316 ■ Open 8am–12:30pm & 5:30–7pm daily

One of Naples' oldest monuments, the church is a mix of Gothic and Baroque styles. The cloister has access to Greco-Roman remains.

2 Gesù Nuovo
MAP N3 ■ Piazza del Gesù 2 ■ Open 7am–1pm, 4–7:30pm daily

The wall of this church dates back to a 15th-century fortified palace. Inside are works of art from the 16th to 19th centuries.

3 San Domenico Maggiore
MAP N2 ■ Vico S Domenico Maggiore 18 ■ Open 10am–1pm & 4–6pm Mon–Fri, 9:30am–6:30pm Sat & Sun

Highlights at this 13th-century church include frescoes by Pietro Cavallini.

4 Sant'Angelo a Nilo
MAP P2 ■ Piazzetta Nilo ■ Open 9:30am–noon daily

This 14th-century church houses the *Assumption of the Virgin* by Donatello.

5 San Gregorio Armeno
MAP P2 ■ Via S Gregorio Armeno 1 ■ Open 9am–1pm & 4:30–7pm Mon–Sat, 9:30am–1pm Sun

This church is best known for the cult of St Patricia, whose blood "liquefies" each Tuesday. It also has a beautiful cloister.

6 San Paolo Maggiore
MAP P2 ■ Piazza S Gaetano 76 ■ Open 9am–6pm & 10am–12:30pm Sun

The 8th-century church still retains two Corinthian columns and features an annexed sanctuary.

7 Santa Maria delle Anime del Purgatorio ad Arco
MAP P2 ■ Via dei Tribunali 39 ■ Open 10am–2pm Mon–Fri, 10am–4pm Sat ■ Adm

The railings outside are adorned with bronze skulls, evoking the tradition of care for the dead.

8 San Pietro a Maiella
MAP N2 ■ Piazza Luigi Miraglia 393 ■ Open 9am–1pm daily

San Pietro underwent a Baroque makeover in the 1600s and then was returned to Gothic style in the 1900s.

9 Santa Maria di Donnaregina Nuova & Vecchia
MAP P1 ■ Vico Donnaregina 26 ■ Open 9:30am–4:30pm (until 2pm Sun); closed Tue

This pair of beautiful churches has been converted into an museum.

10 Santa Maria del Carmine
MAP R3 ■ Piazza del Carmine 2 ■ Open 6:45am–12:30pm & 4:30–7:30pm daily; summer: until 8:30pm daily

Home to the Madonna Bruna icon, the focus of a Naples cult.

Traditional Shops

1 Di Virgilio
MAP P2 ▪ Via San Gregorio Armeno 18

This family-run shop packs a dizzying array of intricate terracotta figures – everything from Pulcinelle to famous footballers.

2 Gambardello Vincenzo
MAP P2 ▪ Via dei Tribunali 90

Take the opportunity to see craftsmen at work at this little *bottega* (workshop), refining the lifelike details of wonderful nativity figures. Most of them are replicas of famous originals, but they will also create personalized versions to order.

3 Melinoi
MAP N3 ▪ Via B Croce 34

An upmarket outlet for stylish clothing, which includes a comprehensive range of choice designer labels from Italy, France as well as Spain.

4 Osmis
MAP N3 ▪ Via Santa Chiara 10F

This little shop carries a charming line of locally and internationally crafted jewellery, masks, lamps, mirrors and candles.

5 Colonnese
MAP N2 ▪ Via San Pietro a Maiella 32-33

One of Naples' most interesting bookstores, with a good stock of rare 18th and 19th century books.

6 Decumano
MAP N3
▪ Via Croce Benedetto 30

This large store specializes in reproductions of various Capodimonte porcelain, as well as other ceramic art from Naples' illustrious past.

7 Via San Sebastiano Shops
MAP N2

Along this street, just off Piazza Bellini, you'll find Neapolitan musical instruments, from mandolins to the *triccaballacco* (a three-pronged clacker with cymbals attached).

Guitars for sale, Via San Sebastiano

8 Tattoo Records
MAP P2 ▪ Piazzetta Nilo 15

In an appealing little piazza just off Spaccanapoli, this funky music shop is good if you're looking for CDs of local music or rare imports. The proprietor will help you find everything from traditional *tarantella* music to the latest Neapolitan rockers.

9 Cosmos
MAP P2 ▪ Via San Gregorio Armeno 5

One of the most inviting shops along this busy shopping street, packed with souvenir-sized lucky charms and pulcinelle.

Porcelain piece, Decumano

10 Scriptura
MAP N2
▪ Via San Sebastiano 22

This small shop sells handmade leather products, including high-quality bags, wallets and diaries. The beautifully packaged items make great gifts to take home.

See map on pp76–7

Old Naples by Night

① Kestè
MAP P3 ▪ Largo S Giovanni Maggiore 26–7

This lively bar with a friendly atmosphere, open every evening for cocktails and beers. It attracts a student crowd, who dance to live bands and spill out onto the square in summer.

② Bar dell'Epoca
MAP N3 ▪ Via Santa Maria di Costantinopoli 82

Tiny place with a few tables along the street. A low-key café by day and one of Piazza Bellini's most popular drinking holes in the evening.

Minimalistic decor at Mamamù

③ La Tana dell' Arte
MAP N2 ▪ Via Bellini 30

Opposite Naples' fine arts academy, the name of this restaurant and cocktail bar means "The Den of Art". The charming setting and outdoor terrace attract an artistic crowd.

④ Galleria 19
MAP N2 ▪ Via San Sebastiano 19 ▪ Closed Sun–Wed & in summer (mid July–mid Sept)

This subterranean club draws a young crowd who come for the DJ-spun mix of house music, electronic sounds and film screenings.

⑤ Evaluna Libreria Cafè
MAP N2 ▪ Piazza Bellini 72

A favourite in the historical centre, this bar-cum-café offers fun and culture to its clientele, who come here to read books and magazines while sipping coffees or cocktails.

⑥ Bourbon Street
MAP N2 ▪ Via Bellini 52 ▪ Closed Mon & Jul–Aug

This large jazz club features local talent every evening. In summer Bourbon Street organizes jazz cruises around the bay.

⑦ Mamamù
MAP P3 ▪ Via Sedile Di Porto 46

A cozy live music venue, this is a hot spot for the young music scene, which showcases indie rock, punk and electric music. Mamamù is frequented by local talents and organizes a popular summer rock festival every June.

⑧ Pepi Vintage Room
MAP N2 ▪ Vico San Domenico Maggiore 23 ▪ Closed Mon

Charmingly casual bar that spills into a narrow alley just below Piazza Luigi Miraglia, with friendly bar staff and creative cocktails. Oddly, they also sell sunglasses.

⑨ Perditempo
MAP N2 ▪ Via San Pietro a Maiella 8 ▪ Closed Sun

This intimate bar-bookshop-music store, located in the historic part of Naples, is anything but a "waste of time" as its name might suggest. An eclectic music soundtrack accompanies the stimulating conversation and good drinks.

⑩ Berisio
MAP N2 ▪ Via Port'Alba 28/29

Established in 1956, this captivating wine bar has vintage, new, old and used books lining the walls. On weekends there is live jazz and blues.

Cafés, Gelaterie and Pasticcerie

1 Gran Caffè Aragonese
MAP N2 ▪ Piazza S Domenico Maggiore 5–8

This café dominates the scene on a crowded piazza. It offers a good range of local desserts and savoury snacks, and excellent Neapolitan-style coffee.

2 Bar Mexico
MAP N2 ▪ Piazza Dante 86

Bar Mexico is reputed to have the best espresso in town, but if you don't want it sweetened (alla napoletana) then ask for a caffè amaro (bitter coffee). A hot-weather winner is the frappe di caffè (iced whipped coffee). You can also stock up on some coffee blends to take home.

3 Spazio Nea
MAP N2 ▪ Via Costantinopoli 53

Located just steps from Piazza Bellini, this contemporary gallery is a gathering spot for artistic types. Overflowing with atmosphere, there's indoor and outdoor seating areas at the lovely café. They also host theatre, peformances and special events.

4 Gay-Odin
MAP N3 ▪ Via B Croce 61

A Naples institution that is a paradise for chocolate lovers. Try the hot chocolate or the divine ice cream.

Gay-Odin chocolate shop

5 Scaturchio
MAP N2 ▪ Piazza S Domenico Maggiore 19

Noted all over Naples for its wonderful traditional pastries, it's a real treat to sample the wares while checking out this piazza. Don't arrive too late or they might have sold out.

Scrumptious pastries at Scaturchio

6 Gelateria della Scimmia
MAP N3 ▪ Piazza Carità 4

This is one of the city's most famous gelaterie (ice-cream parlours) so expect a crowd.

7 Xeo Cafè
MAP N3 ▪ Piazza Sette Settembre 20/21

A bar and gelaterie, here you'll find freshly made, all natural gelato served as ice lollies, which is quite the novelty in Italy.

8 Intra Moenia
MAP N2 ▪ Piazza Bellini 70

A good place to hang out and enjoy a drink. In warm weather it's also a lively gay venue in the evenings.

9 Caffè Arabo
MAP N2 ▪ Piazza Bellini 64

Not just a great café, but a purveyor of tasty Arabic goodies and full meals.

10 Bar Lemmelemme
MAP N2 ▪ Piazza Bellini 74

Another vantage point in Piazza Bellini for an aperol spritz and snacks, while there's a small art gallery on-site.

See map on pp76–7

Pizzerie

1 L'Antica Pizzeria "da Michele"

MAP Q2 ▪ Via Cesare Sersale 1–3
▪ 081 553 92 04 ▪ Closed Mon
▪ No credit cards ▪ €

The most traditional of Naples' *pizzerie*. The menu is limited to only two varieties, *margherita* and *marinara*. Still, the taste is sublime – and the wait often considerable. Take a number at the door before queuing. Tables are shared.

2 Lombardi a Santa Chiara

MAP N3 ▪ Via B Croce 59
▪ 081 552 07 80 ▪ Closed Tue ▪ €
Follow the locals downstairs to eat fresh pizza either standing up or sitting on stools.

3 Di Matteo

MAP P2 ▪ Via dei Tribunali 94
▪ 081 45 52 62 ▪ No credit cards ▪ €
As well as pizza, try some *frittura* here – deep-fried titbits of vegetables, rice and cheese.

4 Pizzeria Dal Presidente

MAP P2 ▪ Via dei Tribunali 120–1 ▪ 081 21 09 03 ▪ Closed Sun
▪ No credit cards ▪ €
Another *pizzerie* on this busy street, which gained its moment of fame when then US President Bill Clinton stopped by for a snack.

5 Pizzeria Starita

MAP M1 ▪ Via Materdei 27–28
▪ 081 557 36 82 ▪ Closed Mon L ▪ €
One of the oldest *pizzerie* in Naples, this place is famous for its *antipasti* and fresh pizzas. The *angioletti fritti* (fried angels) is a popular item, too. Expect a queue, especially weekends.

6 Antica Pizzeria Port'Alba

MAP N2 ▪ Via Port'Alba 18
▪ 081 45 97 13 ▪ €
Through an archway off Piazza Dante, this *pizzerie* even has a traditional wood-fired oven with lava stones from Mount Vesuvius.

7 Pizzeria Trianon da Ciro

MAP Q2 ▪ Via Pietro Colletta
▪ 081 553 94 26 ▪ €
Taking its name from a famous theatre and every bit as traditional as "da Michele" – just across the street – this eatery is more upmarket, with a larger choice. The decor recalls the city's *belle époque* heyday.

Pizzeria Trianon da Ciro

8 Pizzeria Sorbillo

MAP N2 ▪ Via dei Tribunali 32 ▪ 081 44 66 43 ▪ Closed Sun
▪ No credit cards ▪ €
The main restaurant is modern but the stand-up branch next door dates from 1935. Here you can be entertained by pizza makers who twirl the dough, dash on the topping and pop it into the brick oven.

9 Pizzeria Vesi

MAP N2 ▪ Via S. Biagio dei Librai 115 ▪ 081 551 10 35
▪ No credit cards ▪ €
Pizzeria Vesi specializes in "pizza DOC" – a delicious aromatic union of mozzarella balls, *pomodorini* (cherry tomatoes) and basil.

10 Pizzeria Fortuna

MAP R2 ▪ Via PS Mancini 8
▪ 081 20 53 80 ▪ Closed Sun
▪ No credit cards ▪ €
Little more than a counter with a few plastic tables in front, this little place makes delicious *pizzette* and other goodies in seconds.

Restaurants

① Cantina della Sapienza
MAP N2 ▪ Via della Sapienza 40
▪ 081 45 90 78 ▪ Closed D, Sun, Aug
▪ No credit cards ▪ €

The menu changes daily here but is always authentic. Dishes such as *melanzane alla parmigiana* (aubergine/eggplant with mozzarella and tomato) make a regular appearance.

② La Cantina del Sole
MAP P3 ▪ Via G Paladino 3
▪ 081 552 73 12 ▪ Closed Mon, Tue–Sat L, Aug ▪ €

A favourite with the locals, this restaurant is noted for recipes that date back to the 1600s.

③ Bellini
MAP N2 ▪ Via Santa Maria di Costantinopoli 79–80 ▪ 081 45 97 74
▪ Closed Sun D, 1 week in Aug ▪ €€

This *trattoria* specializes in seafood pasta and grilled catch of the day. Pizza also available.

④ Mimì alla Ferrovia
MAP R1 ▪ Via Alfonso d'Aragona 19 ▪ 081 553 85 25
▪ Closed Sun, 2 weeks in Aug ▪ €€

Mimì specializes in fish and seafood, but they also have great *pasta e ceci* (soup with chickpeas).

Seafood dish at Mimì alla Ferrovia

⑤ Palazzo Petrucci
MAP N2 ▪ Piazza San Domenico Maggiore 4 ▪ 081 551 24 60 ▪ Closed Mon L, Sun D ▪ €€€

Neapolitan fare with a creative touch at this Michelin-starred restaurant and adjacent *pizzerie*. Mimimalist decor complements the setting in the stables of Palazzo Petrucci.

⑥ Biancomangiare
MAP M3 ▪ Vico S Nicola alla Carità 13–14 ▪ 081 552 02 26
▪ Closed Sun ▪ €

Taking full advantage of its location next to the market, this family cantina serves fresh fish at great prices.

⑦ Un Sorriso Integrale
MAP N2 ▪ Vico S Pietro a Maiella 6 ▪ €

This vegetarian café serves fresh, healthy meals, including a selection of sharing plates.

⑧ Neapolis
MAP P3 ▪ Via Giovanni Paladino 22 ▪ 081 551 55 84 ▪ No credit cards ▪ €

Cheap and tasty Greek dishes include kebabs and filled pitta breads, which you can eat in or take away.

⑨ Lombardi
MAP P1 ▪ Via Foria 12
▪ 081 45 62 20 ▪ Closed Mon ▪ €€

A rarely crowded restaurant and *pizzerie* with a wonderful antipasto buffet, featuring seasonal delicacies.

⑩ La Locanda del Grifo
MAP N2 ▪ Via Francesco del Giudice 12 ▪ 081 557 14 92 ▪ €€

This *trattoria* and pizzeria serves Neapolitan fare using seasonal produce. The pretty patio overlooks a medieval campanile.

See map on pp76–7 ←

🔟 Toledo to Chiaia

The first impression of the area known as "Royal Naples" is of spaciousness and light. This is Naples' showcase: a vision of

how functional the city can be with due appreciation for its setting. Elegant architecture from various ages graces the terrain here, which is also home to one of the most authentic neighbourhoods, maritime Santa Lucia. Above it all, the Vomero district boasts a fine castle and monastery overlooking the bay and one of the city's best parks, while to the west is the lively Mergellina district, with its working port and busy restaurants lined up along the coast.

Detail on the Triumphal Arch, Castel Nuovo

TOLEDO TO CHIAIA

1 Top 10 Sights *see pp87–9*	**1** Nightlife *see p92*	
1 Places to Eat *see p93*	**1** Performing Arts Venues *see p90*	
1 Shopping *see p91*		

0 metres   500
0 yards   500

San Francesco di Paola

exudes the delicacy of the early Renaissance (see pp14–15). Inside, the spartan blankness is relieved by the ceiling of the Barons' Hall, while the fresco fragments and sculptures in the chapel juxtapose with the harsh reality of the dungeons. In addition there are fine collections of religious and secular artwork. Go up to the battlements to see the panorama.

① San Francesco di Paola
MAP M6 ■ Piazza del Plebiscito ■ Open 8am–noon, 4–8pm daily (to 6pm in winter)

The impetus to build this imitation Pantheon (see p44) came from the Napoleonic king Joachim Murat (1808–15). Completed under the reinstated Bourbon dynasty, the idea was to do away with the chaotic jumble around the palace by recreating a version of the ancient Roman temple to the gods and setting it off with arcades echoing those of St Peter's. It dominates a semicircular piazza with the Palazzo Reale at the opposite end.

② Palazzo Reale
The Royal Palace is largely 18th-century in character, with its vast layout, imposing façade and important rooms such as the ballroom and the chapel (see pp12–13). However, later embellishments took a Neo-Classical turn, in particular the marvellous grand staircase. Under Napoleonic rule many of the rooms received a thorough makeover, which dominates the decor today. Don't miss the fine Renaissance and Baroque paintings from the royal collection, including works by Guercino, Spadarino and several Flemish masters.

③ Castel Nuovo
This rather sombre fortress is a study in stylistic contrasts – in direct opposition to its bulky grey towers, the marble Triumphal Arch

④ Certosa e Museo di San Martino
If there is one place that could be called the true museum of Naples, this former monastery is it. So varied are the collections and the architecture that all aspects of the city's history and cultural output seem to be represented here (see pp26–9). These include a large collection of Nativity scenes, some of Naples' most significant paintings and sculptures, views of the city painted in different eras, a decorative arts collection, and the exuberantly Baroque church, decorated by the best Neapolitan artists of the 17th and 18th centuries.

Stunning ceiling frescoes, Certosa di San Martino

Galleria Umberto I

5 Galleria Umberto I
MAP N5 ■ Piazza Trieste e Trento to Via Toledo

Part of the Urban Renewal Plan following the cholera epidemic of 1884, this space is home to buildings with Neo-Renaissance embellishments and marble floors, overarched by a roof of iron and glass. Located across from the Royal Palace and Teatro San Carlo, the spot immediately became popular with the city's smart and artistic set, and even today has an air of bygone charm.

6 Castel dell'Ovo
MAP K2 ■ Via Partenope ■ Open Jun–Sep: 9am–7:30pm Mon–Sat, 9am–2pm Sun; Oct–May: 9am–6:30pm Mon–Sat, 9am–2pm Sun

In ancient times, this spot was part of the vast estate of the Roman general Lucullus. At the end of the 5th century an order of monks founded a monastery here, then the Normans built the first castle. It was modified by succeeding dynasties, achieving its present form in the 16th century. Legend has it that its name derives from a hidden magic egg (*uovo*), supposedly placed there by the Roman poet Virgil. The building is now used for cultural events.

7 Villa Comunale
MAP K6 ■ Via Caracciolo ■ Open May–Oct: 7am–midnight daily; Nov–Apr: 7am–10pm daily

Designed by Luigi Vanvitelli and inaugurated in 1781 as the royal gardens, this public park is on the bay. It had 19th-century copies of Classical statuary, and was once home to the ancient Farnese Bull group, now in the Museo Archeologico (see p20). Other adornments include a Neo-Classical aquarium; an iron and glass bandstand; and a zoological station with a turtle rescue centre.

Castel dell'Ovo

⑧ Teatro San Carlo

MAP N5 ▪ Via San Carlo 98F
▪ 081 797 23 31 ▪ Open for guided
tours 10am–5:30pm Mon–Sat (to
2pm Sun) ▪ Adm

Built by order of King Charles, this
opera house predates the La Scala
in Milan by some 40 years. Officially
opened on 4 November 1737, it is
one of the most important opera
houses in the world. The interior was
originally in the Bourbon colours
(silver, gold and sky blue), but after
being rebuilt following a fire in 1816
the colour scheme is now mostly
gold and red, though no less
sumptuous. The theatre contains
a museum charting its history.

Auditorium, Teatro San Carlo

⑨ Museo Nazionale della Ceramica Duca di Martina

MAP J4 ▪ Villa Floridiana,
Via Cimarosa 77 ▪ Open 8:30am–
2:30pm Wed–Mon ▪ Adm

Since 1927 this villa (see p49) has been
home to a collection of European and
Oriental decorative art donated by the
Duke of Martina. Of the 6,000 items,
highlights are Hispano-Moorish lustre-
ware, Italian majolica tiles and
18th-century Oriental porcelain.

⑩ Castel Sant'Elmo

MAP L4 ▪ Via Tito Angelini 22
▪ Open 8:30am–6pm daily (museum:
closed Tue) ▪ Adm

This Angevin castle dating from 1329
was upgraded to its six-point con-
figuration in the 16th century, giving
it a militaristic presence looming
above the city. It now houses libraries,
cultural activities and exhibitions.

A DAY IN ROYAL NAPLES

▶ **MORNING**

Begin your tour inside **Galleria
Umberto I**, where you can enjoy
one of Naples' iconic pastries at
Sfogliatella Mary (No. 66) and get
a sense of the bustling optimism
of 19th-century Naples. Coming
out onto Via San Carlo, the
elegant Neo-Classical façade of
the **Teatro San Carlo** is directly
across the street.

Go to the right and around the
corner into Piazza del Plebiscito.
On your right is the massive
dome of the church of **San
Francesco di Paola** (see p87),
and on your left, **Palazzo Reale**
(see pp12–13). First walk over
to the church, noting the bronze
equestrian statues of kings
Charles III and Ferdinand I, then
go back across the piazza to the
Royal Palace. Enter the courtyard
and take the magnificent staircase up to the apartments.

Take a break for a snack or lunch
at the historic **Caffè Gambrinus**
(see p93), just outside the piazza.

AFTERNOON

After lunch go back past the
Teatro San Carlo and the palace
gardens, and be sure not to miss
the giant statues of the horse-
tamers at the gate. Continue on
down and across the lawns to the
Castel Nuovo (see pp14–15). Your
visit here should include the views
from the parapets.

Finally, head up Via Medina to
the **Caffetteria Medina** (see p93),
where you can enjoy a drink while
admiring the Fountain of Neptune.

See map on p86 ⬅

Performing Arts Venues

1 Associazione Scarlatti
MAP L6 ▪ Piazza dei Martiri 58
▪ 081 40 60 11 ▪ www.associazione
scarlatti.it

The best of Naples' small musical companies, it hosts classical chamber music and the occasional jazz group. A typical evening might feature the music of Debussy, Ravel, Chausson and Frank. Venues change frequently.

2 Augusteo
MAP M5 ▪ Piazza Duca d'Aosta
263 ▪ 081 41 42 43 ▪ www.teatro
augusteo.it

Musical comedies are a speciality at this theatre. It also offers shows outside the usual season of October to May. Come here to see contemporary productions, in line with the centuries-old tradition of comic theatre in Naples.

3 Galleria Toledo
MAP M4 ▪ Via Concezione a
Montecalvario 36 ▪ 081 42 50 37
▪ www.galleriatoledo.info

This modern theatre offers avant-garde local works and new international fringe and experimental plays, translated into Italian.

4 Teatro Stabile
MAP N5 ▪ Piazza Municipio 1
▪ 081 551 33 96/03 36 ▪ www.teatro
stabilenapoli.it

Opened in 1779, this historic theatre hosts productions touring Italy.

5 Politeama
MAP M6 ▪ Via Monte di Dio
80 ▪ 081 764 50 01 ▪ www.teatro
politeama.it

This large, modern space offers productions of international music, dance and drama. Performers have included German dancer Pina Bausch and US composer Philip Glass.

6 Nuovo San Carluccio
MAP K6 ▪ Via S Pasquale a
Chiaia 49 ▪ 081 410 44 67

Small companies gravitate here, alternating with cabaret shows.

7 Teatro Nuovo
MAP M4 ▪ Via Concezione a
Montecalvario 16 ▪ 081 497 62 67
▪ www.teatronuovonapoli.it

Fringe, experimental and the best of new international theatre is the keynote at this theatre.

8 Centro di Musica Antica Pieta de' Turchini
MAP M5 ▪ Via S Caterina da Siena 38
▪ 081 40 23 95 ▪ www.turchini.it

In a deconsecrated Baroque church, the Orchestra Cappella della Pieta de' Turchini performs classical music of mostly Neapolitan composers.

9 Teatro Bellini
MAP N2 ▪ Via Conte di Ruvo
14-19 ▪ 081 949 12 66 ▪ www.teatro
bellini.it

Bellini offers mainstream theatre, as well as international and local musicals and concerts. Productions have included *Fiddler on the Roof* and Prokofiev's *Romeo and Juliet*.

Gold and red triumphs, Teatro Bellini

10 Sannazaro
MAP M5 ▪ Via Chiaia 157
▪ 081 41 17 23/ 081 41 88 24
▪ www.teatrosannazzaro.it

This lovely theatre dating from 1874 features its own company, often performing works in Neapolitan dialect.

Shopping

Prints for sale at Bowinkel

1 Bowinkel
MAP N6 ▪ Via S Lucia 25

One of Naples' finest dealers of old books and prints. Expect to find Italian prints that are centuries-old as well as more modern ones, and a host of other Neapolitan memorabilia.

2 Marinella
MAP L6 ▪ Riviera di Chiara 287

This workshop has crafted elegant silk ties, scarves and shoes for over a century. The prices certainly reflect the quality of craftsmanship and the shop's renown.

3 Palazzo Cellamare
MAP L5 ▪ Via Chiaia 149E

Naples' most exclusive tailoring services, specializing in bespoke suits and requiring appointments. They also have ready made clothes.

4 Fusaro
MAP M5 ▪ Via Toledo 276 ▪ Piazza Dante Alighieri 76/77

This local chain specializes in designer gear for men – shoes, suits, shirts and ties, jeans and jackets, as well as caps, bags and belts.

5 Rebecca
MAP L6 ▪ Via Sta Caterina a Chiaia 10–11

With a presence in nearly 30 countries around the world, Rebecca offers stylish jewellery at affordable prices. Silver and gold are featured, with an emphasis on modern pieces compatible with today's taste.

6 Restauro Lepre
MAP K6 ▪ Via Carlo Poerio 80

One of Chiaia's best antique shops, Restauro Lepre has furniture, figurines and other bits and bobs all made to shine by a skillful, friendly, father-and-son duo.

7 Fratelli Tramontano
MAP M5 ▪ Via Chiaia 143

Italians are known the world over for their leather goods, including bags and shoes. Traditional Neapolitan craftsmanship is the byword here.

8 Cameo de Paola
MAP L3 ▪ Via Annibale Caccavello 67/691

This is one of several coral and cameo shops in the vicinity, boasting a vast selection of pieces, some at highly affordable prices.

9 Guarracino Ciro Antichita
MAP L6 ▪ Via Vannella Gaetani 26

This long-time antique store near Piazza dei Martiri deals in furniture, paintings and other pieces of art from the Baroque era through to the 20th century.

10 Dolce & Amaro
MAP M5 ▪ Via Chiaia 160

Thirty-five types of chocolate await you here. Treats include *limoncello*-flavoured dark chocolate and chocolate Neapolitan landmarks, such as Vesuvius. Or how about an all-chocolate coffee-maker with all-chocolate cups?

See map on p86

Nightlife

1 Al Barcadero
MAP N6 ■ Banchina Santa Lucia 2 ■ Open May–Sep

This bar captures the charm of the Santa Lucia quarter, immortalized in one of the most famous Neapolitan songs. By the water, near Castel dell'Ovo, it's great for hanging out and enjoying the views.

2 Vanilla Café
Via Partenope 12

Perfectly situated on the seashore, this trendy bar-café offers great views of the Bay of Naples. Large crowds flock in for its famous aperitifs, especially during summer, adding to the lively vibe.

3 Camarota Spritz
MAP M4 ■ Vico Lungo Teatro Nuovo 31 ■ Closed Mon

Perhaps the most down-to-earth bar in town, serving €1 spritz as well as limoncello and wine. It is popular among students and forms a lively gathering spot at night.

4 S'move
MAP L6 ■ Vico dei Sospiri 10A ■ Closed Aug

Another chic venue, but less pretentious. Although there's no dance floor, the good selection of music keeps things moving.

The bar at S'move

5 Enoteca Belledonne
MAP L6 ■ Vico Belledonne a Chiaia 18 ■ Closed Aug

Shelves of wine bottles lining the walls and a rustic decor provide a perfect backdrop for this trendy wine bar. An extensive wine list and light fare is on offer.

6 66 Fusion Bar
MAP L6 ■ Via Bisignano 58

With an impressively stocked bar, this nightlife spot in Chiaia is popular with locals for its inventive cocktails and lively atmosphere. Excellent wines are available and there is an outdoor seating area.

7 Blue Around Midnight
MAP K3 ■ Via G Bonito 32A

This live jazz venue focuses on standards and classics most of the time, booking well-known performers from around Italy.

8 Macho Lato
MAP K1 ■ Via Abate Minichini 62 ■ Open Sat & Sun only

Attracting an open-minded and diverse gay crowd, this club offers two levels with dancing, lounging and entertainment. Cover charge.

9 Ba-Bar
MAP L6 ■ Via Bisignano 20

For an elegant evening out, head to the stylish Chiaia neighbourhood where locals go for an evening *aperitivo* or dinner and drinks. The French bistro atmosphere, friendly service, extensive wine list and international beer selection make this lively night spot stand out.

10 Discoteca il Fico
MAP K2 ■ Via Tasso 466

A villa dating from the 1800s is the fine setting for this chic disco bar. During the summer months when the weather is fine, the scene moves outdoors to the terrace from where there are great views of the Bay of Naples and Mount Vesuvius.

Places to Eat

1 Caffè Gambrinus
MAP M5 ▪ Via Chiaia 1–2 ▪ €€

This *belle époque* institution still retains much of its original decor. Popular with free-thinking intellectuals and writers, it was closed down by the Fascists as a result. The pastries and buffet lunch are good.

Elegant dining at Caffè Gambrinus

2 Caffetteria Medina
MAP P4 ▪ Via Medina 32 ▪ €€

The café's main claim to fame is its location right next to the Neptune Fountain. Tables outside provide you with an excellent vantage point.

3 Pintauro
MAP N4 ▪ Via Toledo 275 ▪ €

This traditional *pasticceria* (pastry shop) is an ideal choice for procuring the signature Neapolitan sweets, such as *sfogliatella* and *babà (see p67)*.

4 Cavoli Nostri
MAP N6 ▪ Via Palepoli 32 ▪ €€

This stylishly minimalistic restaurant is one of Santa Lucia's more recent additions, with a purely vegetarian menu, including vegan tiramisu.

5 Brandi
MAP M5 ▪ Salita Sant'Anna di Palazzo 1 ▪ 081 41 69 28 ▪ Closed Mon ▪ €€

A Naples institution, laying claim to having invented the pizza margherita during a visit from Italy's Queen Margherita in 1889. Full restaurant menu, too. Reservations essential.

PRICE CATEGORIES

For a three-course meal for one with half a bottle of wine (or equivalent meal), taxes and extra charges.

€ under €30   €€ €30–€50   €€€ over €50

6 LUISE Partenope
MAP M4 ▪ Via Partenope 7 ▪ 081 764 25 63 ▪ €

A small deli offering fried food delights such as *pizza fritta*, *arancini* (fried rice balls) and a selection of pasta and meat dishes.

7 Sfogliatella Mary
MAP M5 ▪ Via Galleria Umberto I 66 ▪ Closed Sun ▪ €€

On the corner of busy Via Toledo, this is among the best places in Naples shell-shaped pastries.

8 Rosati
MAP M4 ▪ Via Chiaia 260 ▪ 081 42 16 86 ▪ €€

Popular for traditional Neapolitan cuisine served at lunchtime.

Pizza from Rosati

9 Osteria da Tonino
MAP K5 ▪ Via Sta Teresa a Chiaia 47 ▪ 081 42 15 33 ▪ Closed Mon April-June ▪ No credit cards ▪ €€

Excellent dishes here include seafood stew. Always lively.

10 Ciro a Mergellina
MAP K2 ▪ Via Mergellina 21 ▪ 081 66 99 28 ▪ No credit cards ▪ €€

Excellent seafood and pasta combinations draw a loyal following.

See map on p86

TOP 10 Vesuvius and Around

Few places on earth are as awe-inspiring as this area of southern Italy. Here lies the heart of Campania, where high culture and the violence of nature have met again and again. Although many lost their families, homes and lives, mankind has ironically gained from these deadly encounters with the mighty volcano that is Mount Vesuvius – in the very act of destruction entire cultures have been preserved for posterity. Here is the city of Pompeii, the town of Herculaneum, and other amazing villas – all of them replete with art and architecture that reveal to us the great heritage of beauty bequeathed by our forebears from Roman times. In later centuries, the unearthing of these treasures inspired kings to build sumptuous palaces, so that they could sample firsthand the exciting discoveries.

Roman mosaic, Herculaneum

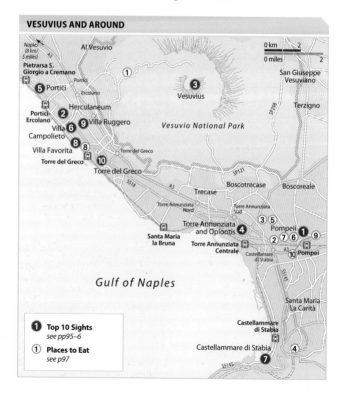

VESUVIUS AND AROUND

Naples (8 km/ 5 miles)

Al Vesuvio

Pietrarsa S. Giorgio a Cremano

⑤ Portici

Portici

Portici-Ercolano

② Herculaneum

Villa ⑥ Campolieto

⑨ Villa Ruggero

③ Vesuvius

Ercolano

Vesuvio National Park

⑧ Villa Favorita ⑧

Torre del Greco

Torre del Greco

⑩ Torre del Greco

San Giuseppe Vesuviano

Terzigno

Trecase

Boscotrecase

Boscoreale

Torre Annunziata Nord

Torre Annunziata and Oplontis ④

Santa Maria la Bruna

Torre Annunziata Sud

③ ⑤

Pompeii ❶ ⑨

② ⑦ ⑥

Torre Annunziata Centrale

Castellammare di Stabia

⑩ **Pompei**

Santa Maria La Carità

Gulf of Naples

Castellammare di Stabia

Castellammare di Stabia ⑦

0 km   2
0 miles   2

❶ **Top 10 Sights**
see pp95–6

① **Places to Eat**
see p97

The ancient city of Pompeii in the shadow of Mount Vesuvius

① Pompeii

Discovered by accident in the 1590s, certainly no archaeological find is more important than that of ancient Pompeii , where a culture was captured forever by the eruption of Mount Vesuvius in AD 79 *(see pp30–31)*. Not only can we see the streets, buildings, furnishings, art, tools, jewellery, and even the food and drink of the people who lived here, but plaster casts reveal the people themselves. From the ruling class down to slaves, we can see their last moments during those terrible few hours that doomed the city.

② Herculaneum

This town, largely a resort in ancient times located right on the sea, was also buried alive by mud and lava from Vesuvius *(see pp32–3)*. Fortunately, wooden structures and other perishable materials were preserved under the lava. However the excavations began in the 18th century when the science of archaeology had yet to be developed, so diggers were not very careful, being mostly on a royal treasure hunt for statuary, mosaics and fresco paintings

③ Vesuvius

MAP D3 ■ Adm ■ www.
parconazionaledelvesuvio.it
Continental Europe's only active volcano has not blown up since its last rumble in 1944, but experts say it could happen at any time; an invigorating hike around the crater is certainly a memorable experience. Today, the volcano inspires both fear and fascination and it is constantly monitored for activity. From the parking lot at the end of the road it is a 30 minute walk along a gravel path to the summit, which affords glimpses into the crater as well as magnificent views around the bay.

④ Torre Annunziata and Oplontis

Few places present such a stark contrast to the visitor as this one *(see pp32–3)*. The contemporary squalor of uncontrolled urban blight hides, within its depressed grime, imperial splendours of the ancient world. Just two blocks from the train station lie the beautifully preserved ruins of one of the most sumptuous villas to have been preserved by Vesuvius's eruption.

Villa Sabina Poppaea, Oplontis

5 Reggia di Portici
MAP L2 ■ Reggia di Portici, Via Università 100 ■ 081 253 20 16 ■ Open 3–6:30pm Thu, 9:30am–6:30pm Fri–Sun ■ Adm

This 18th-century Reggia (palace) of King Charles III and Queen Maria, designed by Antonio Medrano, was the first and greatest of the Vesuvian Villas, the rest of which were built by other members of the Bourbon court. These villas were once left in neglect, however, restoration efforts of the past few years have brought back some of their grandeur

6 Villa Campolieto
MAP L2 ■ Corso Resina 283, Ercolano ■ Open 10am–1pm Tue–Sun ■ Guided tours ■ Adm

This stupendous villa was designed by the Vanvittelli brothers between 1760–75. It features a circular portico, where concerts are held, and enjoys a lovely panorama of the bay. Some of the rooms have been restored to their original decor, while others are used for special exhibitions.

7 Castellammare di Stabia
This port town has been known since ancient times for its thermal springs – the many different waters are each thought to be therapeutic in specific ways (see p33). As with its neighbours, its beauty has been compromised by poverty and developers, but it is not without charm. Nearby, the ruins of aristocratic villas, Arianna and San Marco, offer glimpses into wealthy lifestyles of 2,000 years ago.

Castellammare di Stabia

THE GOLDEN MILE

The 18th-century evolution of *Il Miglio d'Oro* can be traced back to Maria Amalia Cristina, Queen of Naples (**below**). She had grown up in a Viennese palace adorned with two marble statues unearthed at Herculaneum. When she arrived in Naples, she wanted a palace near the site. It started a trend among the nobility and some 120 villas were built.

8 Villa Favorita
MAP L2 ■ Corso Resina 291, Ercolano ■ Open 10am–1pm Tue–Sun

Set in an extensive park, Villa Favorita was boarded up at least 100 years ago. With Italian Unification the noble homes became an obsolete symbol of decadence. However the park and the annexe are open to visitors, the former punctuated with pavilions.

9 Villa Ruggiero
MAP L2 ■ Via A Rossi 40, Ercolano ■ Open 10am–1pm Tue–Sun

Set back from the sea, this house was built in the 18th century for the Baronial Petti family. It has been restored, with Rococo decorations, frescoes and marble busts.

10 Torre del Greco
MAP L3

Set midway between Naples and Pompeii and just beneath the slopes of Vesuvius, this town has been home to coral and cameo artisans for centuries, a craft that still draws admirers today.

Places to Eat

PRICE CATEGORIES

For a three-course meal for one with half a bottle of wine (or equivalent meal), taxes and extra charges.

€ under €30   €€ €30–€50   €€€ over €50

① Kona, Ercolano
MAP L2 ▪ Via Osservatorio 14 ▪ 081 777 39 68 ▪ Closed D daily, except Sat evening ▪ €€

Surrounded by gardens and with a view of the Gulf of Naples from the terrace, dining here is a tranquil experience. Seafood specialities and traditional pasta dishes make up the menu; the fresh seafood salad comes recommended.

② Ristorante Suisse, Pompei
MAP E4 ▪ Piazza Porta Marina Inferiore ▪ 081 862 25 36 ▪ €€

Of all the eateries outside the main gate of the ruins, this one offers the nicest atmosphere. It has indoor and outside tables, and serves a good standard of *trattoria* fare.

③ Zi Caterina, Pompei
MAP E4 ▪ Via Roma 20 ▪ 081 850 74 47 ▪ €

Seafood is a speciality here; try *seppie con finocchi e olive* (cuttlefish with fennel and olives). The wine list features local vintages.

④ Grand Hotel La Medusa, Castellammare di Stabia
MAP E4 ▪ Via Passeggiata Archeologica 5 ▪ 081 872 33 83 ▪ €€

This elegant hotel has a large dining room offering set meals, as well as *à la carte* selections.

⑤ Nuovo Ristorante Anfiteatro, Pompei
MAP E4 ▪ Via Plinio 9 ▪ 081 850 60 42 ▪ €€

Located immediately outside the excavations, this restaurant has been running since 1922. The fresh fish is a good choice in summer.

⑥ Todisco
MAP E4 ▪ Piazzale Schettini 19 ▪ 081 850 50 51 ▪ Closed Mon ▪ €

Friendly, affordable canteen in the centre of town, offering a very authentic dining experience.

⑦ President, Pompei
MAP E4 ▪ Piazza Schettini 12/13 ▪ 081 850 72 45 ▪ Closed Mon ▪ €€€

Located a few meters from the archaeological site of Pompeii, high quality ingredients and cuisine with fresh takes on traditional recipes and an elegant dining space earned this husband-and-wife duo a Michelin star. There is also an excellent wine list to boot.

Il Principe, Pompei

⑧ Osteria del Porto, Torre del Greco
MAP D3 ▪ Via Spiaggia del Fronte 8 ▪ 081 012 53 30 ▪ Closed Tue ▪ €

Seafood restaurant by the port, serving fresh catch and fine desserts.

⑨ Tubba Catubba, Ercolano
MAP D3 ▪ Corso Resina 302 ▪ 081 344 35 03 ▪ Closed Mon ▪ €€

Situated just next to the ruins, this place offers catch of the day and excellent homemade dishes.

⑩ Osteria Da Peppino
MAP E4 ▪ Via Duca d'Aosta 39 ▪ 081 850 48 21 ▪ Closed Tue ▪ €

Alfresco dining under trellis draped by vines and a reasonably-priced menu.

See map on p94

TOP 10 The Islands, Sorrento and the South

This is one of the world's most intensely emotive zones, where verdant-crowned cliffs plunge into the blue sea. On these islands is where the Greeks first brought their high culture to the area, where Roman emperors lived in stupendous luxury, and where, in more recent times, the world's most glamorous celebrities indulged in their own lavish lifestyles. When the American writer John Steinbeck first saw the Amalfi Coast he was moved to uncontrollable weeping. He was not the first – nor will he be the last – to succumb to the emotional impact of the area's potent beauty.

Forio town on the cliffs of the island of Ischia

THE ISLANDS, SORRENTO AND THE SOUTH

1 Ischia
MAP B4

The island of Ischia is surmounted by an extinct 788-m (2,585-ft) volcano, Monte Epomeo, and the many hot mineral springs here (some of them radioactive) have drawn cure- and pleasure-seekers to their soothing sources since ancient times. Green and rugged in appearance, the island also benefits from fine, long beaches. Like Capri, Ischia has had its share of famous residents – in the 19th century the Norwegian playwright Henrik Ibsen wrote *Peer Gynt* during a stay here, while in the 20th century the English poet W.H. Auden and his homosexual circle scandalized the locals. The island was also the first place in the area to be colonized by the Greeks, in the 8th century BC.

2 Paestum
These ancient Greek temples are among the most complete – and most evocative – to have survived into modern times, even taking into

Remains of a Greek temple, Paestum

account those in Greece itself. Besides the beauty and majesty of these timeless structures, this site has offered up countless other treasures, the remains of the Greco-Roman city that thrived here for some 1,000 years. The wonderful on-site museum is the repository of many unique finds, including the only known Greek paintings to have survived the ages. Taken from a tomb found nearby, the frescoes include a depiction of a joyous banquet of lovers, *(see pp38–9)* and a renowned diver – possibly a metaphor for the Greek conception of the afterlife.

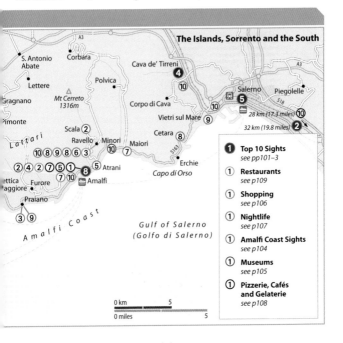

The Islands, Sorrento and the South

	Top 10 Sights
①	see pp101–3
①	**Restaurants** see p109
①	**Shopping** see p106
①	**Nightlife** see p107
①	**Amalfi Coast Sights** see p104
①	**Museums** see p105
①	**Pizzerie, Cafés and Gelaterie** see p108

0 km — 5
0 miles — 5

3 Procida
MAP B4

Smaller than Capri and Ischia and much less touristy, Procida attracts holiday-makers looking for tranquility and cultural tradition. The island has highly fertile soil and is noted for its lemons, considered the best in the region. The island's most original feature, however, is its unique architecture. The colourful houses along the Chiaiolella Port, Marina Corricella and Marina di Sancio Cattolico are known for their vaults – built as winter boat shelters – arches and external staircases.

Colourful buildings, Procida

4 Cava de' Tirreni
MAP F4 ■ Abbey: Open 8am–noon, 4–5:30pm daily; must be booked (347 194 69 57)

In a mountainous valley north of the Amalfi Coast, this town was put up in the Middle Ages thanks to the Benedictine abbey Badia della Santissima Trinità (Abbey of the Holy Trinity) founded in 1011. A visit to the abbey and the medieval Borgo Scacciaventi in the town's centre is an evocative walk through time.

5 Salerno
MAP F4 ■ Duomo: Piazza Alfano I ■ Open 8:30am–8pm Mon–Sat, 8:30am–1pm & 4–8pm Sun

Though the city has largely been ignored by the tourism industry, extensive restoration work on the historic centre has ignited some interest. The Romanesque Duomo is a reminder that Salerno was the capital of southern Italy in the 11th century.

HIKING SPOTS

This region retains a great deal of virtually untouched natural beauty. On Capri, one of the best hikes is up the Scala Fenicia to Anacapri and then on up to the top, Monte Solaro. On Ischia, head up Via Monterone or Via Bocca from Forio, through the Falanga Forest to the summit of Monte Epomeo. Along the Amalfi Coast, the Sentieri degli Dei, above Positano, from Montepertuso to Nocella, offers stupendous views.

6 Sorrento
MAP D5

Palisades and grand hotels notwithstanding, there is no getting around the fact that Sorrento can be chaotic. Yet the town has been a resort since the 1700s – Casanova and Goethe are two notable past visitors – and there is certainly plenty of charm to be found in the old streets.

7 Capri
The fabled isle has had its detractors – it has been called "nothing more than a rocky cliff with over-priced cafés" – and, in ancient times, the notorious shenanigans of Tiberius gave it an enduring reputation as the ultimate in decadence, as did the party life here in the 1950s. Yet, if you choose to stay awhile, you will discover the real Capri beyond the hype – a world of traditional farm life, scenic hiking terrain and sparkling azure waters for swimming and boating. A place with undeniable allure (see pp34–5).

Faraglioni rocks, Capri

⑧ The Amalfi Coast
MAP E5

The famed Costiera Amalfitana lives up to the highest expectations. The winding corniche road offers striking panoramas, and some of the towns seem to defy gravity, clinging to steep slopes. Beauty and history are everywhere, with the most popular destinations being the towns of Amalfi, Positano and Ravello (see pp36–7). The beaches are rocky yet undeniably beautiful, and time spent discovering this perpendicular paradise never fails to delight.

The town of Amalfi, Amalfi Coast

⑨ Massa Lubrense
MAP D5

To the west of Sorrento, this is one of several fishing villages clustered around little ports. Rarely crowded, the site affords wonderful views across to Capri from the belvedere in Largo Vescovado. At Marina di Lobra there's a beach.

⑩ Nerano
MAP D5

This quiet fishing village, close to the tip of the peninsula, offers a peaceful escape. While administratively part of Massa Lubrense on the northern side of the peninsula, its remote location on the southern side means fine views and a scenic beach in the seaside hamlet of Marina del Cantone. With an atmospheric setting, sophisticated seaside dining, and fine hiking along the rugged coastline, including the protected nature reserve at Punta Campanella, it's a lovely spot to while away an afternoon on the Amalfi Coast.

A DAY'S ISLAND HOPPING

▶ MORNING

The tour begins on the island of **Procida**. To get there, take either the first hydrofoil from Naples-Beverello (40 min) or the first ferry from Pozzuoli (30 min) You will arrive at Marina Grande, greeted by the sight of fishing boats and the colourful houses lining the port. Take a quick hike to the island's highest point, the Terra Murata ("walled town").

Back down on the marina, enjoy some refreshment at **Bar Capriccio** (Via Roma 99) while waiting for your hydrofoil to **Ischia** (see p101).

On Ischia you will arrive at Casamicciola, the island's second port, where you can have lunch (Fri–Sun) at the wonderfully rustic **Il Focolare** (Via Cretajo al Crocefisso 3).

AFTERNOON

After lunch take a tour around the island in a glass-bottom boat (departs 2:30pm), stopping at the town of Sant'Angelo. Here you can take in the views, lounge by the dockside or walk along the cliff above Maronti Beach.

At the end of your tour, you can opt to stay over in one of the hotels in Casamicciola, or take a hydrofoil back to the mainland. If you spend the night, the next morning take the hydrofoil or one of the ferries to **Capri** (see pp34–5). After riding the funicular up to Capri Town, follow the signs up to the ruins of Villa Jovis for the breathtaking views.

See map on pp100–1

Amalfi Coast Sights

Positano, climbing up the hillside

1 Positano
Known for decades as a playground for the rich and famous, this is a vertical town in shades of pink and other faded pastels *(see pp36–7)*. Only one street snakes its way through the village - the only way to reach the beach and the heart of the village is to take the steps down.

2 Scala
MAP E5
This lesser-known, tranquil village *(see pp36–7)* sits across the valley from Ravello. The best view of Ravello is from Scala, which is also the starting point for hikes to Amalfi and the Valle delle Ferriere.

3 Praiano
MAP E5 ■ Grotta dello Smeraldo: open Apr–Oct: 9am–4pm daily, Nov–Mar: 9am–3pm daily; adm ■ 089 83 15 35
This little fishing village is perched on a ridge. Further along, you come to the Grotta dello Smeraldo (Emerald Cave). A lift takes you down to the boats to enter the grotto. The cave is also accessible by boat from Amalfi.

4 Amalfi
Amalfi is the largest and most historic town on its eponymous coastline *(see pp36–7)*. Between the 9th and 12th centuries the republic was at its height of mercantile power and the architecture still evokes that glory. The Duomo (cathedral) is glorious.

5 Atrani
MAP E5
■ San Salvatore de' Bireto
This little town exudes a quiet charm, with its arcades and a maze of alley-stairways. Amalfi's doges received their investiture at its church, San Salvatore de' Bireto.

6 Ravello
In the 13th century, Ravello was an important player in the sea trade *(see pp36–7)* as well as the medieval look accounts for its captivating beauty.

7 Minori and Maiori
MAP E5
Maiori has the coast's longest beach, *(see p105)* while Minori has the archaeological site, the Villa Romana.

8 Cetara
MAP F4
Home to the coast's most active fishing fleet, it is also the place to buy *colatura di alici*, a fish sauce descended from the ancient Roman *garum*. A tuna festival takes place every year in early August.

9 Vietri sul Mare
MAP F4
Vietri is universally known for its ceramics, which had begun in the 1400s and are still masterly handcrafted and hand-painted.

10 Conca dei Marini
MAP E5
Known for the luminous light at the Grotta dello Smeraldo (Emerald Grotto), but linger a little longer to see the picturesque marina, 16th-century watchtower and views from the San Pancrazio Church.

Museums

① Certosa di San Giacomo, Capri

MAP U2 ▪ Viale Certosa ▪ 081 837 62 18 ▪ Open 9am–2:30pm Tue–Sun ▪ Adm

This 14th-century monastery features North African-style vaults forming little domes. It now houses a permanent exhibition of Diefenbach paintings.

② Arsenale Museum, Amalfi

MAP E5 ▪ Largo Cesareo Console 3 ▪ 089 87 11 70 ▪ Open 10am–1pm & 4–8pm daily ▪ Adm

This museum traces the history of the Republic of Amalfi and its contributions to the development of the compass and maritime laws.

③ Villa San Michele, Anacapri

MAP S1 ▪ 081 837 14 01 ▪ Open Mar: 9am–4:30pm; Apr & Oct: 9am–5pm; May–Sep: 9am–6pm; Nov–Feb: 9am–3:30pm ▪ Adm

This villa *(see p35)* contains marbles and furnishings from the 17th to 19th centuries.

Ancient statues at Villa San Michele

④ Castello Aragonese, Ischia

MAP B4 ▪ 081 99 28 34 ▪ Open Mar–Nov: 9am–7:30pm ▪ Adm

In the 16th century poetess Vittoria Colonna held court here *(see p131)*, making Ischia the cultural centre of the Mediterranean. Part of the ruin is now the Il Monastero hotel.

⑤ Casa Rossa

MAP T1 ▪ Via G. Orlandi 78 ▪ 081 838 2193 ▪ Open Apr, May & Oct: 10am–4pm Tue–Sun; Jun–Sep: 10am–1:30pm & 5:30–8pm ▪ Adm

Casa Rossa houses local art and is notable for Roman statues from the Blue Grotto.

⑥ Abbazia di San Michele Arcangelo, Procida

MAP B4 ▪ Via Terra Murata 89 ▪ 081 896 76 12 ▪ Open 10am–12:45pm Mon, 10am–12:45pm, 3–5pm Tue–Sat ▪ Adm (donation €2)

This 11th-century abbey is known for paintings by pupils of Luca Giordano.

⑦ Museo Antiquarium Equano, Vico Equense

MAP D4 ▪ Casa Municipale, Via Filangieri 98 ▪ Open 9am–1pm Mon–Fri (also 3:30–6:30pm Tue & Thu); 9:30am–12:30pm Sat

Finds from this Roman town consist of pottery, figurines and tools.

⑧ Correale di Terranova, Sorrento

MAP D5 ▪ Via Correale 50 ▪ 081 878 18 46 ▪ 9:30am–6:30pm Mon–Fri, 9:30am–1:30pm Sat ▪ Adm ▪ www.museocorreale.it

In this 18th-century villa, archaeological finds include a 4th-century BC Greek original of Artemis on a Deer.

⑨ Museo Archeologico Georges Vallet, Piano di Sorrento

MAP D5 ▪ Via Ripa di Cassano 14 ▪ 081 808 70 78 ▪ Open 9am–7pm Tue–Sun

This museum boasts finds from all over the peninsula, including pottery and weapons.

⑩ Villa Romana, Minori

MAP E5 ▪ Via Capodipiazza 28 ▪ Open 8am–1 hour before sunset

In this villa the fresco style dates from the 1st century AD. Excavated artifacts are also displayed here.

See map on pp100–1

Shopping

① Sandalmakers, Capri
Canfora: MAP U1; Via Camerelle 3 ■ L'Arte del Sandal Caprese di Antonio Viva: MAP T1; Via G Orlandi 75, Anacapri

Cobblers jollier than these would be hard to find. Stop by to pick out designs you like and within a few hours – unless you choose something extra fancy – you'll have your hand-tooled, made-to-measure sandals.

Carthusia on Capri

② Carthusia, Capri
MAP C5 ■ Via Camerelle 10

The closest you can come to bringing the natural beauty of Capri home is with Carthusia's collection of perfumes inspired by and created on Capri. Fragrances, soaps and home scents make beautiful gifts.

③ Corallium, Anacapri
MAP T1 ■ Via G Orlandi 50A

A coral and cameo factory in Ercolano. The selection is extraordinary, created with both silver and gold, and prices are excellent. A certificate of guarantee comes with every purchase.

④ Limonoro, Sorrento
MAP D5 ■ Via S Cesareo 51

One of the top souvenirs from the area is *limoncello*, the signature lemon liqueur. This is a good place to watch it being made, after

which you'll understand why it packs such a punch – it's basically pure alcohol with flavouring.

⑤ Salvatore Gargiulo, Sorrento
MAP D5 ■ Via Fuoro 33

Examples of Sorrentine *intarsia* (marquetry) are to be seen all over town, but this workshop turns out top-quality products at reasonable prices. Note the music boxes.

⑥ Ceramiche Tavassi, Anacapri
MAP T1 ■ Via G Orlandi 129

Some of the best ceramics on the island. Designs tend to evoke the natural hues of the setting – azure, gold, green – usually with flowers and vines or other florid vegetation. Anything can be designed to your specifications and you can watch the artists at work.

⑦ La Scuderia del Duca, Amalfi
MAP E5 ■ Cesareo Console 8

Amalfi's handmade paper-making tradition is vibrantly on display in this beautiful shop.

⑧ Camo, Ravello
MAP E4 ■ Piazza Duomo 9

A cameo factory (and museum) that sells cameos and coral jewellery.

⑨ Ceramiche d'Arte Carmela, Ravello
MAP E4 ■ Via dei Rufolo 16

This workshop is the place to come for gorgeous ceramics decorated with traditional designs.

⑩ Milleunaceramica, Amalfi
MAP E5 ■ Via Pietro Capuano 36

This shop is a treasure trove of locally produced ceramics. Each piece is handpicked by the owner and created by artisans.

Milleunaceramica

Nightlife

1 Taverna Anema e Core, Capri

MAP U1 ■ Via Sella Orta 1 ■ Closed Oct–Mar: Mon–Fri

The "Soul and Heart" taverna is still redolent of *la dolce vita* vibes of decades past and is considered Capri's premier nightclub. It attracts a chic, yet fun-loving crowd.

2 Number Two, Capri

MAP U1 ■ Via Camerelle 1

Another hot spot and local celebrity hangout. The DJ spins cool house and techno dance music, but don't get here before 2am. Dressy club attire is *de rigueur*.

3 Qubè Café, Capri

MAP U1 ■ Via li Curti 6

A quirky disco-bar a short stroll from Capri's stylish Piazzetta. With a local feel that's a refreshing change from the island's posh night spots, music varies from classic rock to electronic.

4 Discoteca Valentino Pianobar, Ischia

MAP B4 ■ Corso Vittoria Colonna 97

This tired and ageing club still attracts a young, energetic crowd.

5 Chaplin's Pub, Sorrento

MAP D5 ■ Corso Italia 18

A delightful mix of Irish and Italian, this friendly, family-owned Irish pub in the heart of Sorrento offers an excellent beer selection.

6 Music on the Rocks, Positano

MAP E5 ■ Grotta dell'Incanto 51 ■ Closed mid Sept-Mar

Evocatively set inside a cavern, this beachside disco pub is the hot spot for nightlife on the Amalfi Coast. At weekends it is a high-energy nightclub featuring international DJs and live music. Cover charge.

La Piazzetta, the social heart of Capri

7 La Piazzetta, Capri

MAP U1

Capri Town's main square may be small but it's big on *la vita mondana* (sophisticated lifestyle). The little bars, with their cluster of outdoor tables, are a magnet for daytrippers and locals alike, although the latter generally turn up after dark when the former have moved on.

8 Annunziata Church, Ravello

MAP E4 ■ Via della Annunziata ■ www.ravelloarts.org

Dating from the Middle Ages, this church is no longer used for religious services; the Ravello Concert Society presents year-round chamber concerts in this evocative setting.

9 Africana, Marina di Praia

MAP E5 ■ Via Terramare 2

The approach to this disco is via a walkway cut out of a seafront rock face, while the dance floor seems to be suspended above the waves. Decor includes ethnic masks and parrots.

10 Villa Rufolo, Ravello

MAP E4 ■ Piazza Duomo ■ Open 8am–8pm in summer, 9am–4pm in winter

Jazz concerts and classical recitals are held in the grounds of the Villa Rufolo from June to September.

See map on pp100–1

Pizzerie, Cafés and Gelaterie

① Gran Caffè, Amalfi

MAP E5 ▪ Corso delle Repubbliche Marinare 37/38 ▪ €€

With picturesque outdoor seating overlooking the beach and port of Amalfi, this café is a popular spot with locals and visitors for enjoying drinks or a light meal. The sunset views are spectacular.

Relaxing on the piazza outside Pasticceria Pansa

② La Zagara, Positano

MAP E5 ▪ Via dei Mulini 10 ▪ €

La Zagara is a major tourist magnet, but there's no denying that the treats they turn out here are delicious: pastries, cakes, fresh fruit sorbets and the like. The patio, with fragrant lemon trees, is captivating.

③ Bar Tiberio, Capri

MAP U1 ▪ La Piazzetta ▪ €€

One of the main bars on the Piazzetta, but everyone has his or her own favourite. Great for people-watching.

④ Bar Calise, Ischia

MAP B4 ▪ Piazza degli Eroi 69 ▪ €

One of the island's best bars, with excellent *gelato* (ice cream) and *dolci* (desserts). It's surrounded by dense greenery in the middle of a traffic circle in this laid-back port.

⑤ Da Maria, Amalfi

MAP E5 ▪ Via Lorenzo d'Amalfi 14 ▪ 089 87 18 80 ▪ Closed Mon ▪ €€

Amalfi's best wood-fired pizza can be found at this friendly place near Piazza Duomo. Local specialities also feature on the menu.

⑥ Villa Verde, Capri

MAP U1 ▪ Via Sella Orta 6/a ▪ 081 837 70 24 ▪ €€€

Offering spacious indoor seating as well as a lush garden, this restaurant has exquisite *focaccia* and pizza and an excellent house red from Calabria.

⑦ Pasticceria Pansa, Amalfi

MAP E5 ▪ Piazza Duomo 40 ▪ €

An Amalfi institution since 1830, this elegant bar offers a wide selection of irresistible sweets and locally made chocolates. The chocolate covered citrus peels are a treat. Outdoor tables provide a view of the goings-on in the main square.

⑧ Da Pasquale, Sant'Angelo, Ischia

MAP B4 ▪ Via Sant'Angelo 79 ▪ 081 90 42 08 ▪ €€

Dining is home-style here, even to the occasional sharing of tables and bench seating. The pizza is tasty and there's a good choice of beer and wine.

⑨ Sant'Antonino, Sorrento

MAP D5 ▪ Via Santa Maria delle Grazie 6 ▪ 081 877 12 00 ▪ €€

Excellent, wood-fired pizza is served here for lunch and dinner. The heat of traditional wood ovens flash-bakes the dough, preventing the toppings from becoming soggy.

⑩ Nonna Sceppa, Paestum

MAP H6 ▪ Via Laura 53 ▪ 082 885 10 64 ▪ Closed Thu (winter only), Oct ▪ €€

The least touristy of the choices here is a highly recommended restaurant that turns out excellent pizzas, as well as seafood and other home-style dishes. Wild mushrooms in season – try some on your pizza.

Restaurants

1 La Cambusa, Positano
MAP E5 ▪ Piazza Vespucci 4
▪ 089 87 54 32 ▪ Closed winter ▪ €€

Positioned to the right of the beach, with dining on a porticoed balcony. Seafood is the thing to go for.

2 Marina Grande, Amalfi
MAP E5 ▪ Via della Regione 4
▪ 089 87 11 29 ▪ €€

One of the best restaurants in town, right on the sea. Dishes include seafood ravioli with *arugula* (rocket) sauce.

3 Villa Maria, Ravello
MAP E4 ▪ Via Santa Chiari 2
▪ 089 85 72 55 ▪ €€€

With a breathtaking setting and pergola-covered dining terrace, this is a peaceful respite for savouring the views and Ravello specialities.

4 Buca di Bacco "da Serafina", Capri
MAP U1 ▪ Via Longano 25
▪ 081 837 07 23 ▪ Closed Wed ▪ €€

This place is top of most locals' list, for both quality and price. Cooking features seafood, *antipasti* and pizza.

5 Da Paolino Lemon Trees, Capri
MAP C5 ▪ Via Palazzo e Mare 11
▪ 081 837 61 02 ▪ €€€

Enjoy romantic outdoor dining under the lemon trees at this country-style restaurant. Traditional Caprese dishes are as luscious as the setting.

Da Paolino Lemon Trees, Capri

6 Terrazza Bosquet, Sorrento
MAP D5 ▪ Grand Hotel Excelsior Vittoria, Piazza Tasso 34
▪ 081 877 71 11 ▪ €€€

The grandest experience Sorrento has to offer, in the frescoed dining room of this superlative hotel. Silver, china, crystal and fine linen complement the service you receive.

7 Il Solitario, Anacapri
MAP T1 ▪ Via G Orlandi 96
▪ 081 837 13 82 ▪ €

This delightful place is like being in someone's private garden. Everything is homemade and the freshest the season has to offer.

8 La Conchiglia, Chiaia Beach, Procida
MAP B4 ▪ Steps from Via Pizzaco 10
▪ 081 896 76 02 ▪ Closed Nov–Mar ▪ €€

Get here by walking down 183 steps from Piazza Olmo or reserve a boat trip from Corricella. Try the pasta with sweet mussels and courgettes (zucchini).

9 Alberto al Mare, Ischia
MAP B4 ▪ Via Cristoforo Colombo 8 ▪ 081 98 12 59 ▪ €€

Located over the water, the bounty of the sea is the speciality here. Options might include swordfish or monkfish.

10 Don Alfonso 1890, Sant'Agata sui Due Golfi, Sorrentine Peninsula
MAP D5 ▪ Corso Sant' Agata 13
▪ 081 878 00 26 ▪ Closed Mon, 7 Jan–7 Mar ▪ €€€

With two Michelin stars expect lavish elegance and impeccable food. The tasting menus and their accompanying wines are superb.

See map on pp100–1

🔟 Posillipo, Pozzuoli and the North

If central seaside Naples is known as "Royal Naples", the coastal area to the west could be called "Imperial Naples" for its enormous popularity with imperial families and their courtiers in ancient Roman times. Significant ruins left by them are everywhere hiding behind the postwar *abusivo* (illegal) building developments that now blot the landscape. However, the area is subject to one of nature's stranger phenomena, called Bradyseism – underground volcanic activity gives rise to "slow earthquakes", resulting in the continual rising and lowering of the land, making it an unstable base for settlement. The region is relatively unexplored by modern-day tourists but was top of the list for those who took the 19th-century Grand Tour, not least because it includes one of Italy's finest palaces, the Reggia di Caserta.

Royal throne, Reggia di Caserta

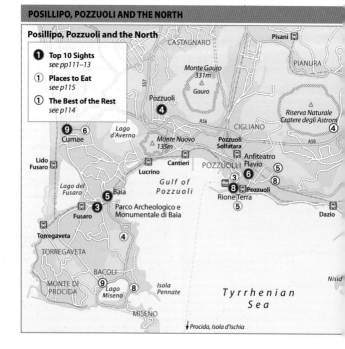

POSILLIPO, POZZUOLI AND THE NORTH

Posillipo, Pozzuoli and the North

① **Top 10 Sights** see pp111–13
① **Places to Eat** see p115
① **The Best of the Rest** see p114

CASTAGNARO
Pisani
PIANURA
Monte Gauro 331m
Gauro
SS7
Pozzuoli ④
A56
CIGLIANO
Riserva Naturale Cratere degli Astroni ④
A56
⑨ ⑥ Cumae
Lago d'Averno
Monte Nuovo 135m
Pozzuoli Solfatara
Lido Fusaro
Cantieri
Lucrino
POZZUOLI
Anfiteatro Flavio ⑤
Lago del Fusaro
Baia ⑤
Gulf of Pozzuoli
③ ⑥ ⑧
⑧ Pozzuoli
Rione Terra ⑤
Dazio
③ Fusaro
Parco Archeologico e Monumentale di Baia
Torregaveta
④
TORREGAVETA
BACOLI
MONTE DI PROCIDA
⑨ Lago Miseno
⑧ Isola Pennate
Nisid
Tyrrhenian Sea
MISENO
↓ Procida, Isola d'Ischia

View from Parco Virgiliano

1 Parco Virgiliano
MAP J3 ■ Viale Virgilio
■ Open May & Jun: 7am–midnight;
Jul–Sep: until 1am; Oct–Apr: until 9pm

Occupying the summit of a hill, this park has amazing views. Below lies the island of Nisida, formed from an ancient volcanic crater and connected by a causeway.

2 Marechiaro
MAP J2

One of the most romantic spots on this evocative coastline, this little fishing village is dotted with ancient ruins and restaurants with great views (see p61). The panoramic vista of Vesuvius from here is repeatedly celebrated, most nostalgically in the quintessential song 'O Sole Mio.

3 Parco Archeologico e Monumentale di Baia
MAP B3 ■ Via Sella di Baia 22, Bacoli
■ 06 399 67 050 to book
■ Open 9am–1 hour before sunset
Tue–Sun ■ Adm €4 (combined fare for 3 other Phlegrean fields sites
■ www.coopculture.it

Arranged in terraces, this excavated area has an ancient spa and a Temple of Diana. The spa complex comprises baths named after Venus and Mercury, the latter a large swimming pool once covered with a dome.

4 Pozzuoli
MAP C3

Called Puteoli by the Romans, this seaside town was a major player 2,000 years ago. Ruins here include the archaeological site of Rione Terra the excavation of which has made exciting progress in recent years, and the Serapeum, thought for centuries to be a temple of the Egyptian god Serapis but now known to have been one of the empire's largest markets. Puteoli was the main imperial port and retained its importance even after the Port of Ostia was upgraded by Emperor Trajan in the 2nd century.

Archaeological site at Pozzuoli

5 Baia
MAP B3 ■ Museo Archeologico dei Campi Fiegrei (06 399 67 050) ■ Adm

This town was the most sumptuous resort of the ancient world. Due to seismic activity in this area, it is now a unique flooded city that can be explored by dives or by boat (see p63). There's also a 15th-century castle here, the Castello di Baia, housing an archaeological museum, while to the north is Lago d'Averno, a crater lake that the ancients believed marked the entrance to the Underworld. To the east of town is the Villa Volpicelli, appearing like a floating castle along the edge of Lago del Fusaro.

Anfiteatro Flavio

Underwater city, Baia

THE BURNING FIELDS

Flegrei and Phlegrean derive from a Greek word *phlegraios* (burning), applied in ancient times to this zone of perpetual, low-level volcanic activity. **(below)** Below the earth's surface here, magma (molten rock) is flowing, applying pressure upward, making it one of the most unstable regions of the earth's crust, literally littered with volcanic cones and craters.

6 Anfiteatro Flavio
MAP C3 ■ Corso Terracciano 75 ■ 081 526 60 07 ■ Open 9am–1 hour before sunset Wed–Mon (Oct–May until 2pm) ■ Adm

This is the third-largest Roman amphitheatre in the world, after those at Rome and Capua – again making it clear how important this area was to the empire. It seated 40,000 and was equipped with an array of below-floor apparatus for making the *venationes* (wild animal "hunts") that took place as theatrical as possible. Nowhere are such systems so well preserved, due to the lower portion of the structure having been buried until modern times.

7 Capo Posillipo
MAP J2

The ancient Greeks called the area Pausilypon ("respite from pain") due to the great beauty of the place. Through the ages, it retained its appeal due to a succession of inhabitants and visitors, from religious communities in medieval times to holiday resorts for the Spanish aristocracy in the 17th century. The Spartan years of the 1950s, however, put an end to that famous beauty in large swaths with the unregulated spread of ugly apartment buildings. Fortunately, parts of the area down by the water still retain great charm.

8 Rione Terra

MAP C3 ▪ Largo Sedile di Porta ▪ 081 853 0626 ▪ Tours at 11am, 12pm, 2:20pm & 4:20pm daily (40 minutes each) ▪ Adm

This excavation site continues to reveal the remains of a Roman settlement underneath the abandoned Spanish town on the hilltop. After exploring the Roman streets, you'll emerge at the baroque Cathedral of San Procolo, supported by the giant columns of the long-hidden Temple of Augustus.

9 Cumae

MAP B3 ▪ Via Montecuma ▪ Open 9am–1 hour before sunset daily ▪ Adm

Founded in the 8th century BC, Cumae played a big part in history (see p63), due to its seeress. The Cumaean Sibyl, priestess of Apollo, was an oracle who exerted great influence, and leaders of Rome depended on her prophecies. Sibyl's Grotto, with its weird trapezoidal entrance tunnel, is an enigmatic experience.

Italian gardens, Reggia di Caserta

10 Reggia di Caserta

MAP D1 ▪ Via Douhet 22 ▪ 0823 44 80 84 ▪ Palace apartments: open 8:30am–7:30pm Wed–Mon; park: open 8:30am–1 hour before sunset Wed–Mon ▪ Adm ▪ www.reggia dicaserta.beniculturali.it

Neapolitan Baroque at its most refined, this 18th-century palace is set around four courtyards with lavish rooms, highlighted by the Great Staircase and the Throne Room. The park has huge decorated fountains, culminating in the Grande Cascata.

A MORNING IN ANCIENT POZZUOLI

▶ Start the tour in the cool of the morning with a visit to **Solfatara** (see p114), the vast volcanic lava cap about 1 km (0.5 mile) north of the town. This stark, bizarre site will set the tone for the day's musings on the ephemeral nature of all things. Next, head back towards town on the Via Vecchia di San Gennaro and take a quick left on Via Domiziana, which follows the ancient Roman road of basalt stones built to link Rome to Puteoli (Pozzuoli; see p111). Visit the **Santuario di San Gennaro** (see p114) and see the spot where Naples' patron saint met his martyrdom under Emperor Diocletian.

From here, turn back and go down Via Vecchia di San Gennaro to the Piscina Cardito, a 2nd-century cistern with a vaulted ceiling supported by pillars. Continue on to the great **Anfiteatro Flavio** and try to imagine what it might have been like, with full scenery and exotic beasts springing out of trapdoors. Next, follow Via Terracciano along to the Terme di Nettuno, huge terraced baths, and on the opposite slope the Ninfeo di Diana, a fountain that may have been part of the baths.

Work your way down towards the ancient port, most of it now underwater, to the Serapeum (market). Then walk up onto the promontory, the **Rione Terra**, to explore the 2,000-year-old Duomo (cathedral).

🍴 Finally, enjoy a well-deserved lunch at the **Antica Trattoria da Ciuffiello** (see p115).

See map on pp110–11

The Best of the Rest

(1) Science City, Bagnoli
MAP J2 ▪ Via Coroglio 104
▪ 081 735 22 20/22 ▪ Open 9am–2pm
Mon–Sat; 10am–6pm Sun ▪ Adm
▪ cittadellascienza.it

This hands-on science centre (see p64)
is designed to educate and amuse
kids of all ages.

(2) Santa Maria del Faro, Posillipo
MAP J2 ▪ Via Marechiaro 96a
▪ 081 769 14 39 ▪ Open during services

Dating back to the 1300s, this church
was probably built over the remains
of a Roman *faro* (lighthouse). It was
restored in the 18th century.

(3) Museo Provinciale Campano di Capua
MAP C1 ▪ Via Roma 68 ▪ 082 396 10 42
▪ Open times vary, check website
▪ Adm ▪ www.museocampano.it

The wealth of ancient Capua is on
display in this museum.

(4) Cratere degli Astroni
MAP C3 ▪ Via Agnano Astroni
468 ▪ 081 588 37 20 ▪ Open Mar–Nov:
9.30am–1hr before sunset Fri–Sun
▪ Adm

The Romans tapped the geothermal
properties of this volcanic crater to
build their spas.

(5) Solfatara, Pozzuoli
MAP C3 ▪ Via Solfatara 161
▪ 081 526 23 41/74 13 ▪ Open 8:30am–
6pm daily ▪ Adm ▪ www.solfatara.it

Above the town, this crater of
a dormant volcano presents
an unearthly landscape.

Volcanic landscape at Solfatara

(6) Palazzo Donn'Anna, Posillipo
MAP J2 ▪ Piazza Donn'Anna 9
▪ Closed to the public

The air of mystery that envelops this
17th-century palace has given rise to
rumours. One claims Queen Joan II
used it for illicit trysts, after which she
had her lovers tossed into the sea.

(7) Benevento
MAP F1

This town's pride and joy is the well-
preserved Arch of Trajan, chronicling
the Roman emperor's civic works.

Arch of Trajan, Benevento

(8) Santuario di San Gennaro, Pozzuoli
MAP C3 ▪ Via S Gennaro Agnano 10
▪ 081 526 11 14 ▪ Open 9am–noon,
4:30–7pm daily; closed Fri morning

This 16th-century church is said to
mark the spot where Naples' patron
saint was decapitated, and the brown
stain on a stone is said to be his blood.

(9) Bacoli
MAP B4 ▪ Via A Greco 10 ▪ Open
9am–1 hour before sunset daily

Noteworthy here is the *Piscina Mirabile*,
a cistern used to collect water for the
old port of Misenum.

(10) Santa Maria Capua Vetere
MAP C1

Livy observed in the 1st century BC
that Capua was the "biggest and
richest city in Italy". It is now home
to a ruined amphitheatre and a
fascinating ancient temple.

Places to Eat

PRICE CATEGORIES

For a three-course meal for one with half
a bottle of wine (or equivalent meal),
taxes and extra charges.

€ under €30   €€ €30–€50   €€€ over €50

1 Gelateria Bilancione, Posillipo

MAP J2 ▪ Via Posillipo 238B
▪ Closed Mon

Take in the vista while enjoying your
favourite gelato at this ice cream shop.

2 Giuseppone a Mare, Posillipo

MAP J2 ▪ Via Russo 13 ▪ 081 769 12
78 ▪ Closed Mon–Thu L, Sun D ▪ €€

Renowned since 1889, the seafood is
excellent. Popular for receptions and
celebrations, so book ahead.

3 Antica Trattoria da Ciuffiello, Pozzuoli

MAP C3 ▪ Via Dicearchia 11 bis ▪ 081
526 93 97 ▪ Closed Mon (winter) ▪ €€

This restaurant is known for its grilled
specialities. Their consummate *zuppa
di pesce* (fish soup) is a meal in itself.

4 A' Casa 'e Tobia, Bacoli

MAP B4 ▪ Via Fondi di Baia 12
▪ 081 523 51 93 ▪ Closed Mon–Tues &
Sun D ▪ €

Wonderful organically grown food,
from the rich volcanic soil of the crater
on which the place is perched. It is
best to book ahead.

5 Da Don Antonio

MAP C3 ▪ Vico Magazzini 20
▪ 081 853 13 37 ▪ Closed Mon ▪ €€

Counted among the best seafood
restaurants lining Pozzuoli's harbour,
Da Don Antonio offers excellent and
reasonably-priced fish pasta dishes.

6 Vinaria, Pozzuoli

MAP C3 ▪ Via Monte di Cuma 3
▪ 081 804 62 35 ▪ Closed Mon–Thu,
Sun D ▪ €€€

This restaurant boasts its own piece of
history with Roman ruins discovered

on site. The wine list highlights
bottles from Camania and those
produced in the Campi Flegrei.

7 Da Teresa, Casertavecchia

MAP D1 ▪ Via Torre 6 ▪ 082 337
12 01 ▪ €

Offers great views over Caserta and
generously portioned set meals of
mountain game or seafood.

8 Féfé, Bacoli

MAP B4 ▪ Via della Shoah 15,
Casevecchie ▪ 081 523 30 11
▪ Closed Mon D (winter) ▪ €€

Filled with regulars, this place
faces the port. You are welcomed
with the house aperitif and advised
of the seafood specials of the day.

9 'A Fenestella, Marechiaro

MAP J2 ▪ Via Marechiaro 23
▪ 081 769 00 20 ▪ Closed Tue ▪ €€

This restaurant offers, alongwith
typical Neopolitan dishes, the
best seafood. You can take in views
of Marechiaro's picturesque harbour.
Save room for the delicious babà!

Pasta Paccheri with Prawns

10 Da Gino e Pina, Benevento

MAP F1 ▪ Viale dell' Università 2
▪ 082 42 49 47 ▪ Closed Sun D, Aug ▪ €

A popular family-run restaurant
serving traditional cuisine using local
produce. Try the homemade pasta in
local saffron liqueur. Good desserts.

See map on pp110–11

Streetsmart

Elegant shopping arcades of
Galleria Umberto I, Naples

Getting To and Around Naples and the Amalfi Coast

Arriving by Air

The **Capodichino Airport** in Naples is 5.9 km (3.7 miles) northeast of the city centre. National and international flights arrive from all the main Italian cities and most major European ones.

Alitalia is the main carrier within Italy. Major European airlines offer connections to Naples, including **British Airways**, **Air France**, **Lufthansa** and **Iberia**, as well as low-cost carriers like **easyJet and Ryanair**.

Taxis and car rental companies are located outside the arrivals hall. The regular **Alibus** service runs from the airport to Napoli Centrale train station and Piazza Municipio, giving access to the Naples Molo Beverello for a ferry to Sorrento and the islands. **Curreri Viaggi** also offers a bus service from the airport to Sorrento.

Arriving by Train

The train service to Naples is operated by Italy's national rail comany, **Trenitalia**, and by **Italo**. Naples' main station is called Centrale, which offers connections to local bus and Metro lines, as well as the **Circumvesuviana** train.

Keep in mind that there are no train stations on the Amalfi Coast. The closest is in Salerno, which is serviced by both Trenitalia and Italo. One more option is to take the Circumvesuviana train to Sorrento. From both Salerno and Sorrento there are buses and ferries to various places on the Amalfi Coast.

Arriving by Sea

A very pleasant way of travelling to this part of Italy is by boat. Ferry and hydrofoil services run from Sardinia, Sicily, the Aeolian Islands and many other Mediterranean ports. Cruise ships also make stops in Naples and along the coast.

Arriving by Road

Reaching Naples by car is possible but it is by no means advisable for the uninitiated. As you hit Naples, there are so many perplexing interchanges, with inadequate signage, that it is easy to get lost. Driving along the twisty and narrow Amalfi Coast road is also an adventure. Given the intense driving experience and extremely challenging parking, many travellers prefer to arrive and travel around Naples or the Amalfi Coast by other methods of transport.

Arriving by Bus

The regular bus and coach services are a good way to get to Naples and other towns in the area. If you're arriving in Naples by bus, you will find yourself in one of the main squares, Piazza Garibaldi, in front of the Centrale train station.

Getting Around by Train and Metro

Naples and its vicinity has a complex but reliable transport system (**ANM**), including trams, funicular railways and light railways that serve outlying areas. There is also a Metro system in Naples and most lines converge at the Centrale train station.

The Circumvesuviana train goes to Sorrento, with stops along the way, including archaeological sites such as Pompeii. The Circumflegreo and Cumana trains go west to the Campi Flegrei.

Getting Around by Bus

The city buses in Naples are not for the faint-hearted. The system is chaotic and the old buses are dirty, crowded and subject to traffic jams. Most bus lines have their terminus at Piazza Garibaldi. Buy tickets from any local bar before boarding and validate them once on board. Open-top, hop-on hop-off **City Sightseeing** buses depart from Piazza Municipio and are a fun way to discover Naples, as well as Sorrento and the Amalfi Coast. The Amalfi Coast is also served by the **SITA** bus company.

Getting Around by Boat

Once here, you could stick to ferries, going from port to port (though ferries do not run on the Amalfi

Coast from November to March/April). Naples has two ports, then there are the islands, Amalfi, Pozzuoli, Sorrento, Positano and Salerno. Companies include **Alilauro**, **Caremar**, **SNAV** and **Travelmar**.

Getting Around by Taxi

There are taxi ranks throughout Naples and at the airport. Set fares are in place and a list of tariffs with surcharges must be displayed. A taxi from the airport to the town centre is about €30. Companies include **Consorzio Taxi**, **Consortaxi**, **GESCAB** and **Radio Taxi La Partenope**.

Getting Around by Car

The minimum age for renting a car is 21, but some companies charge extra from people younger than 25. Most companies require that you be covered for any eventual problem, including collision damage and theft.

Getting around by car in Naples and along the Amalfi Coast area is likely to stress even the calmest of drivers (cars are not allowed on Capri). Traffic jams on the Sorrentine Peninsula and the Amalfi Coast are maddening, car theft is common, the motorways are chaotic and confusing, and parking is impossible.

Getting Around by Bicycle and Motorcycle

Navigating the chaotic traffic in and around Naples on two wheels is not recommended. It's possible on the islands of Procida and Ischia, the mountainous backroads along the Sorrentine Peninsula and the Amalfi Coast; but be prepared for narrow roads and surprises at every turn.

Tickets

Unico Campania offers 1-day or weekly tickets for integrated travel in Naples and regional areas in Campania. For the Amalfi Coast, look for the **Unico Costiera** tickets (can be purchased per route) or 1- or 3-day passes. Validate tickets before departure by stamping them in the machine on board.

Getting Around on Foot

Walking is a good way to explore the villages along the Amalfi Coast, which have staircases and narrow alleys. The area is blessed with mountain trails for hiking. Some of them thread their way along old goat paths from village to village.

DIRECTORY

ARRIVING BY AIR

Air France
w airfrance.com

Alibus
w anm.it

Alitalia
w alitalia.it

British Airways
w britishairways.com

Capodichino Airport
w aeroportodinapoli.it

Curreri Viaggi
w curreriviaggi.it

easyJet
w easyjet.com

Iberia
w iberia.com

Lufthansa
w lufthansa.com

Ryanair
w ryanair.com

ARRIVING BY TRAIN

Circumvesuviana
w eavsrl.it

Italo
w italotreno.it

Trenitalia
w trenitalia.com

GETTING AROUND BY TRAIN, METRO AND BUS

ANM
w anm.it

City Sightseeing
w city-sightseeing.it

SITA
w sitasudtrasporti.it

GETTING AROUND BY BOAT

Alilauro
w alilauro.it

Caremar
w caremar.it

SNAV
w snav.it

Travelmar
w travelmar.it

GETTING AROUND BY TAXI

Consortaxi
w consortaxi.com

Consorzio Taxi Napoli
w consorziotaxinapoli.it

GESCAB
w gescab.it

Radio Taxi La Partenope
w radiotaxilapartenope.it

TICKETS

Unico Campania/ Costiera
w unicocampania.it

Practical Information

Passports and Visas

Citizens of the EU can use their national identity cards to enter Italy. Visitors from outside the EU need a valid passport to enter the country. Travellers from the US, Australia, New Zealand, Canada and Japan do not need a visa for stays of up to three months as long as the passport is valid for six months beyond the date of entry. For longer stays, a visa is necessary and can be obtained at the **Ministry of Foreign Affairs** before arrival, and once in Italy you should apply at the local *questura* (police station) for a *permesso di soggiorno*.

Other nationalities should check entry details at their local embassy or consulate. Italian consulates in your home country can be good sources for detailed information, including tourism, employment, and residency in Italy.

Customs and Immigration

Italian customs is run by the **Agenzia delle Dogane e dei Monopoli**. Their "Traveller's Customs Charter" gives details of the import and export regulations. There are no limits for EU citizens on most goods carried in or out of Italy as long as they are for personal use. Travellers can import from EU countries: 800 cigarettes, 400 cigarillos, 1kg (2.2 lb) of smoking tobacco, 10 litres of spirits over 22 per cent proof, 20 litres of alcoholic beverages under 22 per cent, 90 litres of wine (no more than 60 litres of sparkling wine) and 110 litres of beer. Travellers from non-EU countries can import 200 cigarettes, 100 cigarillos, 50 cigars, 250 g of smoking tobacco, 1 litre of spirits over 22 per cent proof, 2 litres of alcoholic beverages under 22 per cent, 4 litres of wine and 16 litres of beer.

Non-EU residents can claim a VAT refund on EU purchases *(see p124)*.

Travel Safety Advice

Visitors can get up-to-date travel safety information from the **Foreign and Commonwealth Office** in the UK, the **State Department** in the US, and the **Department of Foreign Affairs and Trade** in Australia.

Travel Insurance

All travellers are advised to buy insurance against theft or loss, accidents, illness and travel delays or cancellations. Italy has a reciprocal health agreement with other EU countries, and EU citizens are automatically entitled to medical care in Italy if they have a valid European Health Insurance Card (EHIC). Non-EU visitors should check if their country has reciprocal arrangements with Italy.

Health

Italy does not require any vaccinations, and there are few health hazards. Tap water is potable; however, many Italians prefer to drink bottled water.

For minor ailments, look for the green or red cross sign indicating a *farmacia* (pharmacy). Pharmacists in Italy are highly trained and can serve as surrogate doctors, and they can usually prescribe just the right thing if your symptoms are clear. Often, drugs that would require a prescription in your home country can be sold without one in Italy. If you need to fill a specific prescription, it's important to know the actual chemical in question and not just its brand name, as it may be different in Italy. Pharmacies keep regular shop hours, but there will always be at least one in the area that is open outside normal hours. Look for the list posted next to the door of any *farmacia*, which will show the schedule of off-hour openings nearby.

There are hospitals *(see Directory)* covering most of Amalfi Coast, Capri, Ischia, Naples and Sorrento that provide 24-hour emergency care. If you would prefer an English-speaking doctor, contact your country's consulate in Naples for recommended doctors.

Personal Security

Naples' reputation as an unsafe city has improved drastically. However, like any large city it is best to be cautious. Leave all valuables, including your passport, in a hotel safety deposit box. Pickpockets are not uncommon in crowded parts of Naples, particularly on public transport. Keep your valuables tucked away in unreachable places. Carry wallets in front pockets and ensure bags are strapped across your front. In restaurants and cafés, keep your personal belongings on your lap or tied to your person. Losses or thefts should be reported to the nearest police station.

Though petty thievery is part of the scene in Naples, violent crimes are quite rare. Such things generally occur only in the underworld of organized crime far from the regular tourist spots.

Compared to Northern Europe, attitudes towards women travellers can be quite macho in the Naples area. Still, women generally do not encounter excessive harassment and can travel alone without a problem, especially on the Sorrentine Peninsula and the islands. Naturally, it is best for women to exercise normal care, especially after dark. Women shouldn't stay around Naples' central train station if travelling on their own.

Emergency Services

For emergencies, there are dedicated numbers for the **Carabinieri** (police), **State Police**, **Fire Brigade** and **Ambulance**.

Travellers with Specific Needs

Getting around in a wheelchair in Naples and the Amalfi Coast area is a near impossibility without assistance. The larger museums and sights are making some headway at providing easier access. Although progress is slow, things are improving gradually, as more and more places try to upgrade in order to conform to EU standards. Visitors with specific needs will, without a doubt, require help from travelling companions at every stage of their journey.

Many older buildings, which are normally refurbished medieval structures, are often without facilities for wheelchair users – there are endless stairways and levels to contend with, sometimes, even within a single room. The only reliable option is to stay in the newest hotel you can find, where lifts will probably be big enough and bathroom sizes will all comply with EU laws. Double-check the facilities on offer before booking anything.

Currency and Banking

Italy uses the euro (€), which is divided into 100 cents. Paper notes are in denominations of €500, €200, €100, €50, €20, €10 and €5. Coins are €2, €1, 50c, 20c, 10c, 5c, 2c and 1c.

ATMs (called *bancomats* in Italy) are the easiest and safest way to get cash while travelling and are also a way to beat commission charges at *bureaux de change*. Italian ATMs charge no transaction fee; you'll only have your own bank's fee to pay for using a non-branch machine and possibly a foreign transaction fee. If you withdraw the maximum each time (usually €250) the fee will likely be only about 1 per cent. Banks also normally offer better exchange and commission rates than hotels or *bureaux de change*, although rates can vary from bank to bank.

Credit cards are accepted in most large places. Only restaurants and smaller businesses might not, as card companies charge 2–4 per cent commission from them. You may be charged 2 per cent on every card purchase by your bank for currency conversion. If your credit card is lost or stolen, inform the local police and your credit card company immediately.

Telephone and Internet

The dialling code for Italy is 39, and when calling any number in Italy you must include the area code that starts with a zero.

To call outside Italy, dial 00 then the country code, area code and number.

Most mobile phones will work in Italy, but it is advisable to check with your provider before departure. Consider buying a local SIM card to avoid high roaming charges. SIM cards are inexpensive and readily available from cell phone providers: TIM, Wind, Vodafone and Tre.

Free Wi-Fi is available at many hotels, cafés and restaurants. However, smaller hotels may still charge for internet or only provide it in the lobby.

Postal Services

Main branches of Italy's **Poste Italiane** post offices are open 8:20am–7:05pm Tuesday to Friday and 8:20am–12:35pm on Saturdays. In smaller branches, rural towns or villages the post offices will often be open only 8:20am–12:35pm from Tuesday to Saturday. Mailboxes are red and have two slots – one *"per la città"* (local) and one *"per tutte le altre destinazioni"* (everywhere else).

Stamps *(francobolli)* are on sale at post offices and tobacconists *(tabacchi)*, and often (unofficially) at any shop selling postcards.

TV, Radio and Newspapers

Most hotels will have satellite TV and the international news channels that come with it. Many programs on Sky satellite TV channels can be switched to the original language. The popular local radio station in Naples is **Radio Kiss Kiss** (95.9FM).

Newsstands and book sellers stock a selection of Italian and international press. *USA Today* and the *International Herald Tribune* are generally available in tourist areas, along with most major British, German and French newspapers. The local newspaper published in Naples is *Il Mattino*, while the online newspaper **The Local** covers Italian news in English. For events in and around Naples, pick up a copy of the free monthly magazine **Qui Napoli**.

Opening Hours

During August many businesses close mid-afternoon or entirely.

Most shops are usually open from 9am–2pm and 4–8pm, except in popular tourist areas where they will likely remain open through the lunch *riposo*.

Many shops, hotels and restaurants close for part or all of the holiday season, especially on the Amalfi Coast, Capri and Ischia. Banks generally open 8:30am–1:30pm and 3:30–4:30pm from Monday to Friday.

Museums and galleries have their own opening hours which may change with the season, especially in coastal areas and the islands. Museums and historic sites will often close one day per week, even in high season. It is best to check their websites before you visit.

Nearly all banks, shops and businesses are closed on public holidays: New Year's Day, Epiphany (6 Jan), Easter, Easter Monday, Liberation Day (25 Apr), Labour Day (1 May), Republic Day

(2 Jun), Ferragosto (15 Aug), All Saints Day (1 Nov), Immaculate Conception (8 Dec), Christmas Day (25 Dec) and the Feast of St Stephen (26 Dec).

Time Difference

Italy is one hour ahead of Greenwich Mean Time (GMT) and 6 hours ahead of US Eastern Standard Time (EST). The clock moves forward 1 hour for daylight saving time from the last Sunday in March until the last Sunday in October.

Electrical Appliances

In Italy, the electrical voltage and frequency is 220V/50Hz and plugs with two or three round pins are used. Devices from other countries may need adapters and voltage converters.

Weather

The climate is typically Mediterranean, with warm summers and cool winters. July and August are very hot and humid, with temperatures around 20°–30° C (66°–86° F). The best weather is in spring and autumn, from October to December tend to be the rainiest months. Winter is cold, dark and rainy, but can offer dramatic views of Vesuvius's snowy peak.

For culture, visit Naples in the winter, when you'll get a feel for local life and fewer crowds at popular sites. To avoid the crowds for swimming, June or September are a better bet than July and August, which is when most of Italy will be on holiday. To appreciate the natural beauty and the quality of life, any time of year is ideal. Most hotels and restaurants on the Amalfi Coast and islands close for a period or the entire winter.

Visitor Information

Naples has two main **Azienda Autonoma di Soggiorno** (ASST) offices, one near Galleria Umberto I and the other at Piazza del Gesù. Free maps, brochures and information on events and attractions are available in multiple languages. You can also contact the Italian Tourist Board in your home country before your departure.

Along the Amalfi Coast, tourist information offices are located in **Amalfi**, **Positano** and **Ravello**. **Sorrento** and the islands of **Capri** and **Ischia** also have official information offices.

A number of websites can help you research exactly which parts and how much of the fascinating area you want to cover during your visit. A notable example is the **Napoli Unplugged** website, which has detailed information in English on transport, history, events and things to see and do in Naples.

Useful apps include Google Maps, Google Translate, TripAdvisor for restaurant reviews, **Travelmar** for purchasing tickets for ferries along the Amalfi Coast and Gira Napoli for navigating public transport in Naples itself, all available for Android and iOS devices.

DIRECTORY

POSTAL SERVICES

Poste Italiane
w posteitaliane.it

TV, RADIO AND NEWSPAPERS

Il Mattino
w ilmattino.it

The Local
w thelocal.it

Qui Napoli
w inaples.it/ita/quinapoli.htm

Radio Kiss Kiss
w kisskiss.it

VISITOR INFORMATION

Azienda Autonoma di Soggiorno Cura Amalfi
w amalfitouristoffice.it

Azienda Autonoma di Soggiorno Cura Ischia and Procida
w infoischiaprocida.it

Azienda Autonoma di Soggiorno Cura Isola di Capri
w capritourism.com

Azienda Autonoma di Soggiorno Cura Napoli
MAP N5 (081 40 23 94
MAP N3 w inaples.it

Azienda Autonoma di Soggiorno Cura Positano
w aziendaturismopositano.it

Azienda Autonoma di Soggiorno Cura Ravello
w ravellotime.com

Azienda Autonoma di Soggiorno Cura Sorrento
w sorrentotourism.com

Napoli Unplugged
w napoliunplugged.com

Travelmar
w travelmar.it

Trips and Tours

With a wealth of history and culture, there are many different ways to enjoy a visit to Naples. Walking is one of the best ways to explore the city, especially in the historic centre. Get a good introduction to Naples on a walking tour by **Free Walking Tour Napoli**.

A visit to Naples isn't complete without delving into the local cuisine. From making your own Neapolitan pizza to sampling the best sweets, **Eat in Italy** provide cooking lessons and food tours led by experienced locals.

For a more in-depth look at Naples' rich archaeological sites, world-class museums and distinctive culture, **Context Travel** offers unique and highly informative tours led by local historians and academics.

You will see another side of Naples by going underground with **Napoli Sotterranea**. Tours lead far underground and back through history, from Greek-Roman aqueducts to areas used as shelters during World War II.

For local tours in Naples and guided excursions to Pompeii, Capri, Sorrento and the Amalfi Coast, try the family-run company **Rimonti Tours**.

In summer, there is no better way to see the coastline than by boat. Local family-run company **Gennaro e Salvatore** operate personalized tours to admire the beautiful caves and bays, stopping to take a dip here and there.

Shopping

Naples is an excellent shopping destination, with all the big Italian brands represented as well as a large selection of boutiques for designer fashion, accessories and home decor. For upmarket shopping, the Chiaia neighbourhood has the finest selection of designer boutiques. Men's fashion is especially refined in Naples. For more popular brand name shopping, Via Toledo, Galleria Umberto I *(see p88)* and the historic centre are the best bet.

Naples is renowned for its antique and second-hand shops. The best-known antique dealers, such as **Brandi** and **La Florida** can be found at Via Domenico Morelli.

While exploring the Sorrento Peninsula and islands, great buys include locally made ceramics, handmade paper in Amalfi, hand-carved cameos or hand-made leather sandals. You'll also find local wines, cheeses, and the popular *limoncello* liqueur. Check for any restrictions on importing foodstuffs into your home country before you buy.

There are two main sales periods per year that are determined by the Italian government for each region. Summer sales usually start at the beginning of July and run for 60 days. Winter sales begin around Epiphany (6 Jan) and run until March.

Prices include VAT (IVA in Italian), which currently stands at 22 per cent on most purchases. For non-EU residents, VAT refunds are available for purchases over €155 that will be taken outside the EU. You will need to ask the sales clerk for a form or card at the time of purchase (note that not all shops participate in VAT returns). VAT can be redeemed at the customs counter in the airport at your last point of departure from the EU.

Dining

Famous as the birthplace of pizza and many Italian favourites, Neapolitan cuisine is loved around the world. Restaurants in Naples and the surrounding area are primarily dedicated to Neapolitan cooking, and international cuisine options are hard to find. Some pizzerias may offer pasta, meat and fish dishes as well as pizza, but don't be surprised if the most popular serve only pizza – and just a few varieties at that. Yet with such a delightful variety of options, from seafood to delicious meat recipes, it's rarely a problem to find something for every taste.

With an endless variety of traditional Neapolitan vegetable recipes, there is never a shortage of choices on the menu for vegetarians and vegans. Every part of Campania has its own specialities and similar dishes may be interpreted in quite different ways from one location to another.

Restaurants usually open from 1–3pm for lunch and 7–10:30pm for dinner. Italians generally eat dinner from 8–9:30pm, so expect to find the best atmosphere around that time. In popular tourist areas some restaurants may serve continuously. Cafés are often open for light meals throughout the day.

Restaurants rarely have children's menus available, but are usually happy to prepare special pasta dishes for customers. Few restaurants have high chairs, or perhaps just one or two for the entire establishment.

Accommodation

There is something for all tastes and budgets in the Naples and Amalfi Coast area, whether you're looking for five-star luxury, a charming villa rental in a secluded spot or a budget-friendly hostel. In Naples, the most convenient places to stay are in the centre of the city, making them accessible to all the main sights. Naples is also a good base for exploring Pompeii, Vesuvius and the islands (see pp131–2).

The Amalfi Coast and Capri have long held a reputation for being expensive, with many luxurious hotels having taken advantage of the spectacular landscape. You will get what you pay for, however, as service and facilities are of a very high standard. Cheaper alternatives can be found in smaller towns, such as Praiano, but even Positano offer some budget accommodation (see pp130–31).

Sorrento's reputation as a luxury resort is well founded, although there is no shortage of cheaper hotels – you will just find yourself further from the centre of things and with less breathtaking views (see pp129–30).

Rates are the highest during peak season in the summer and during Easter and Christmas. Booking well in advance is recommended for the period from Easter through to October, especially for the Amalfi Coast, Capri and Sorrento. Low season specials are abundant in Naples and shoulder season bargains are sometimes available along the coastal areas and islands. Contrary to the high season rates and crowds in the Amalfi Coast, August can be quieter in Naples with some hotels offering lower tariffs.

EPT, the Italian Tourist Board publishes lists of hotels, pensioni and campsites. You can also make inquiries at the **Associazione degli Albergatori Napoletani** (Neapolitan Hotel Owners' Association). To stay in the countryside in a private home or on a farm, a great option for families, try the **Agriturist** website. Alternatively, to rent an apartment or home in Naples check **Airbnb.**

Most hotels and hostels now have online booking or subscribe to major booking websites. Airbnb, **Booking.com** and **Hotels. com** have extensive listings for Naples and the surrounding areas. It is always worth checking prices at the establishment itself as they often feature offers that are not available on booking websites. **Hostelworld** provides information about the best hostels in Naples, Capri, Ischia, Sorrento and the Amalfi Coast. **Summer in Italy** specializes in holiday villa rentals in Capri, Sorrento and on the Amalfi Coast. If you are looking to stay with private families, **Rent a Bed** offers a range of choices and areas in Naples and on the coast.

DIRECTORY

TRIPS AND TOURS

Context Travel
W contexttravel.com

Eat in Italy
W eatinitaly
foodtours.com

**Free Walking
Tour Napoli**
W freewalking
tournapoli.com

Gennaro e Salvatore
W gennaroesalvatore.it

Napoli Sotterranea
W napolisotterranea.org

Rimonti Tours
W rimontitours.com

SHOPPING

Brandi
Via D Morelli 9–11
☏ 081 551 12 80

La Florida
Via Merliani Giovvani
☏ 081 551 12 80

ACCOMMODATION

Airbnb
W airbnb.com

Agriturist
W agriturist.com

**Associazione degli
Albergatori Napoletani**
W napleshotels.na.it

Booking.com
W booking.com

Hostelworld
W hostelworld.com

Hotels.com
W hotels.com

Rent a Bed
W rentabed.it

Summer in Italy
W summerinitaly.com

Places to Stay

PRICE CATEGORIES

For a standard, double room per night (with breakfast if included), taxes and extra charges.

€ under €150   €€ €150–€300   €€€ over €300

Luxury Hotels in Naples

Costantinopoli 104

MAP N2 ■ Via S Maria di Costantinopoli 104 ■ 081 557 10 35 ■ www.costan tinopoli104.it ■ €€

This stylish hotel, with stained-glass windows and wrought-iron work, is housed in an Art Nouveau villa. Some rooms have a terrace. There is a pool too.

Eurostars Hotel Excelsior

Via Partenope 48 ■ 081 764 01 11 ■ www.euro starsexcelsior.com ■ €€

This *belle époque* palazzo is the grande dame of Naples' plush hotels, and it has seen everyone from celebrated actors to monarchs pass through its elegant doors. Another of the waterfront hotels, Excelsior has command-ing views of the entire bay, Vesuvius and Castel dell'Ovo

Grand Hotel Santa Lucia

Via Partenope 46 ■ 081 764 06 66 ■ www. santalucia.it ■ €€

Though more modest, this hotel has the most character of the three "grands" that stand along the bay. It has views of the Castel dell'Ovo and has a tasteful Art Nou-veau decor, along with all the comforts you may require.

Grand Hotel Vesuvio

Via Partenope 45 ■ 081 764 00 44 ■ www.vesuvio.it ■ €€

Destroyed in World War II and restored to its orig-inal grandeur in the1950s, this hotel consequently lacks the charm of its neighbours, but is still the preferred lodging of many visiting VIPs. It is very well positioned, with views of the Bay of Naples and Vesuvius in the distance.

Hotel San Francesco al Monte

MAP K2 ■ Corso Vittorio Emanuele 328, Vomero ■ 081 423 91 11 ■ www. sanfrancescoalmonte.it ■ €€

A former 16th-century Franciscan monastery where the now-luxurious former monks' cells have views over the bay, and there's a garden restau-rant with more vistas.

Hotel Una

MAP R2 ■ Piazza Garibaldi 9/10 ■ 081 563 69 01 ■ www.unahotels.it ■ €€

Part of a Florentine hotel chain, this restored 19th-century palazzo has a luxury interior with spa-cious rooms. The rooftop bar has great views.

Miramare

MAP N6 ■ Via Nazario Sauro 24 ■ 081 764 75 89 ■ www.hotelmiramare.com ■ €€

Built in 1914 as an aristocratic villa, this modernized hotel has retained its original Art Nouveau style. Located right on the bay, its lovely terrace and many rooms afford spectacular views.

Palazzo Caracciolo

MAP Q1 ■ Via Carbonara 112 ■ 081 016 01 11 ■ www.accorhotels.com ■ €€

This regal hotel was once the home of the aristo-cratic Caracciolo family, where famous guests such as the king of Naples and Napoleon's brother-in-law were welcomed. Near the Duomo, enjoy elegant surroundings and modern comfort in this intimate, upmarket hotel.

Paradiso

MAP J2 ■ Via Catullo 11 ■ 081 247 51 11 ■ www. hotelparadisonapoli.it ■ €€

Paradiso is a Best Western chain hotel but Mediterranean in feel. Perched on Posillipo Hill, it's far from the city chaos and has a terrace restau-rant with a stunning view of Vesuvius.

Grand Hotel Parker's

MAP L4 ■ Corso Vittorio Emanuele 135 ■ 081 761 24 74 ■ www.grandhotel parkers.it ■ €€€

This fine old hotel was a Grand Tour stopover. Restored to its former glory, it boasts antiques, chandeliers and original art. Be sure to visit the wonderful library, full of antiquarian books. There are two restaurants, one with postcard views from the roof garden, and an in-house spa.

Good-Value Hotels in Naples

Hotel Correra 241
MAP N2 ▪ Via Correra 241 ▪ 081 19 56 28 42 ▪ www.correra.it ▪ €
Close to the Museo Archeologico Nazionale, this little oasis can be reached through a gate leading to a discreet doorway. Beyond is a colourful hotel with sunny terrace and large, bright, airy rooms. The breakfast here is good.

Il Convento
MAP M4 ▪ Via Speranzella 137/A ▪ 081 403 977 ▪ www.hotelilconvento.it ▪ €
Small, family-run hotel in the Quartieri Spagnoli, minutes away from the lively pedestrian shopping area of Via Toledo. Il Convento has recently-renovated, bright rooms, some with balconies overlooking the street.

Mercure Napoli Angioino Centro
MAP N4 ▪ Via A Depretis 123 ▪ 081 491 01 11 ▪ www.accorhotels.com ▪ €
Part of a modern international chain, this hotel boasts a pleasant terrace overlooking Castel Nuovo. It is a comfortable choice in Royal Naples.

Neapolis
MAP N2 ▪ Via Francesco del Giudice 13 ▪ 081 442 08 15 ▪ www.hotel neapolis.com ▪ €
Located within the old centre, this friendly hotel offers comfortable, if somewhat spartan, rooms and a cosy communal terrace overlooking the city

Frequent special offers for travellers are available on their website.

Partenope Relais
MAP L6 ▪ Via Nicolò Tommaseo 1 ▪ 081 195 70 632 ▪ €
This boutique hotel has sleek and airy modern rooms – some with sweeping views of the sea – that pay tribute to film stars such as Sophia Loren.

Pinto-Storey
MAP K5 ▪ Via G Martucci 72 ▪ 081 68 12 60 ▪ www. pintostorey.it ▪ €
Dating from 1878 and redolent of bygone days, this hotel is very stylish, with Art Nouveau touches and an overall aura of gentility. It's in one of the nicest parts of town, close to the Villa Comunale. Many rooms have great views of the bay, and air conditioning is available at an extra charge.

Rex
MAP N6 ▪ Via Palepoli 12 ▪ 081 764 93 89 ▪ www.en.hotel-rex.it ▪ €
Rex is located by the sea in a beautiful Art Nouveau style building around the corner from Naples' bastions of luxury. Most of the rooms are decorated with paintings of Naples and have charming balconies with views of Vesuvius. The decor is simple but comfortable, and breakfast is included, served in your room.

Toledo
MAP M4 ▪ Via Montecalvario 15 ▪ 081 40 68 00 ▪ www.hotel toledo.com ▪ €
Located in a restructured 17th-century palazzo, which is in the earthy

Spanish Quarter, the Toledo hotel is situated halfway between Royal Naples and the historic centre. Its location is convenient for tourists as it is near every important monument and is easily accessible by all forms of public transport.

Caravaggio
MAP P2 ▪ Piazza Cardinale Sisto Riario Sforza 157 ▪ 081 211 00 66 ▪ www. caravaggio hotel.it ▪ €€
Housed in a beautifully restored 17th century building in the Tribunali neighbourhood, one of the most evocative parts of the old centre, this hotel exudes style. It's right behind the cathedral.

Chiaia Hotel de Charme
MAP M5 ▪ Via Chiaia 216 ▪ 081 41 55 55 ▪ www. chiaiahotel.com ▪ €€
This very special place actually consists of rooms in the restored palace of a Neapolitan marchese. It's appropriately located in Royal Naples, so that you can indulge all of your aristocratic fantasies. The rooms are full of original furnishings and each is named after one of your host's noble ancestors.

Budget Hotels in Naples

Belle Arti Resort
MAP N2 ▪ Via Santa Maria di Costantinopoli 27 ▪ 081 557 10 62 ▪ www. belleartiresort.com ▪ €
This boutique B&B offers elegant rooms in a convenient location for an attractive price. Some rooms are adorned with beautiful ceiling frescoes from the 17th century.

Europeo

MAP P3 ▪ Via Mezzocannone 109 ▪ 081 551 72 54 ▪ www.hotel europeonapoli.com ▪ €

Situated near Piazza San Domenico Maggiore, this hotel is well placed for checking out the university area and the ancient centre. The rooms have style and some are decorated with wall frescoes. These rooms include breakfast, served on the roof terrace of the nearby Executive Hotel.

Hotel des Artistes and Hostel

MAP P1 ▪ Via Duomo 61 ▪ 081 192 550 86 ▪ www.hoteldesartistes naples.it ▪ €

Set in a period palazzo with a grand entrance and stairway. It is a few blocks from the Museo Archeologico in one direction and the Duomo in the other. Dorm beds are available.

Hostel of the Sun

MAP N4 ▪ Via G Melisurgo 15 ▪ 081 420 63 93 ▪ www.hostelnapoli.com ▪ €

This lively hostel has well-priced dormitories and private rooms, some of which have en-suite bathrooms. Situated near the water, it is a stone's throw from Royal Naples and very convenient for the old centre. The atmosphere is friendly and the staff multilingual.

Hostel-Pensione Mancini

MAP Q2 ▪ Via P S Mancini 33 ▪ 081 553 67 31 ▪ www.hostelpensione mancini.com ▪ €

Located just a 5-minute walk from Centrale train station, this recently refurbished hostel offers both private rooms and dorms. There is free Wi-Fi and a communal kitchen.

Hotel Piazza Bellini

MAP N2 ▪ Via S Maria di Costantinopoli 101 ▪ 081 45 17 32 ▪ www.hotel piazzabellini.com ▪ €

The comfortable rooms feature stylish, private bathrooms and modern decor with wooden floors and colourful artwork on the walls. The hotel is handy for Piazza Bellini and for all the sights of the old centre. A buffet breakfast is included.

Hotel San Pietro

MAP Q3 ▪ Via San Pietro ad Aram ▪ 081 28 60 40 ▪ www.sanpietrohotel.it ▪ €

San Pietro is located in historic Naples near museums, restaurants and the central station. The rooms are well-furnished and clean, and the staff is on call 24 hours a day. There's a pleasant rooftop bar.

La Terrazza

MAP Q2 ▪ Corso Umberto I 190 ▪ 339 543 20 06 ▪ www.bnblaterrazza.it ▪ €

A laid-back B&B that is handy for the historic centre of Naples. It has clean, spacious rooms and a lovely terrace.

Neapolitan Trips

MAP N4 ▪ Via dei Fiorentini 10 ▪ 081 551 89 77 ▪ www.neapolitantrips. com ▪ €

This hotel offers bright, simple rooms in the city centre with a spacious communal terrace. The large yet cosy hostel below, set around a sunny terrace of its own, also has plenty of dorm beds.

Pizzasleep

MAP M2 ▪ Piazzetta Sant' Alfonso e Sant'Antonio a Tarsia 11G ▪ 081 549 6766 ▪ www.pizzasleepbeb.it

With brightly-lit and attractive rooms that boast pretty views over the city, this family-run B&B is set in the quiet streets west of Piazza Dante. Guests receive a very warm welcome from the hosts.

Capri Gems

Villa Eva

MAP S1 ▪ Via La Fabbrica 8, Anacapri ▪ 081 837 15 49 ▪ www.villaeva.com ▪ €

This paradise, close to the Blue Grotto, has an array of bright, uniquely-styled rooms around a pretty garden and pool.*(see p55)*.

Villa Krupp

MAP T2 ▪ Viale Matteotti 12 ▪ 081 837 03 62 ▪ Closed Nov–Mar ▪ www. villakrupp.com ▪ €

Situated above the Gardens of Augustus, this white-washed stone villa used to be Maxim Gorky's house. A more panoramic position would be hard to find, even on this island. Beautifully decorated, in the light-suffused Capri way, with antiques appropriate to its historic importance.

A Pazziella

MAP U1 ▪ Via Fuorlovado 36 ▪ 081 8370642 ▪ www.royalgroup.it/ apazziella/it ▪ €€

The overall impression here is light-filled freshness, cool colours and serenity, yet it's just a few steps away from the high-life in La Piazzetta and the shops and restaurants.

It is a wonderful place for a Capri sojourn.

Bellavista

MAP T1 ▪ Via Orlandi 10, Anacapri ▪ 081 837 14 63 ▪ www.bellavistacapri.com ▪ €€

Vine-covered walkways surround the main hotel building, and the rooms are airy and well-appointed. It is closed between November and Easter.

Weber Ambassador

MAP T2 ▪ Via Marina Piccola ▪ 081 837 01 41 ▪ Closed Nov–Mar ▪ www. hotelweber.com ▪ €€

With its commanding position overlooking this little port and just a few steps away from the beach, this hotel makes a perfect hideaway. The many terraces at several levels afford magnificent views of the famous I Faraglioni rocks.

Capri Palace Hotel and Spa

MAP U1 ▪ Via Capodimonte 14 ▪ 081 978 01 11 ▪ www.capri palace.com ▪ €€€

The level of comfort at the Capri Palace is astounding. The beauty and spa treatments are excellent. There's a large swimming pool and some suites even have their own pools. The hotel's L'Olivo is a Michelin-starred restaurant.

Grand Hotel Quisisana

MAP U1 ▪ Via Camerelle 2 ▪ 081 837 07 88 ▪ www.quisisana.com ▪ €€€

This is the jewel in the crown of Capri exclusivity, opulence, attention to detail and sheer scale.

Restaurant, lounges, private rooms, pools and gardens, are all serenely beautiful.

Hotel Caesar Augustus

MAP T1 ▪ Via G Orlandi 4, Anacapri ▪ 081 837 33 95 ▪ Closed Nov–mid-Apr ▪ www.caesar-augustus. com ▪ €€€

The Caesar Augustus takes its rightful place among the finest accommodation options in the world. Its terrace dazzles with its position above the bay.

JK Place Capri

MAP U1 ▪ Via Marina Grande 225 ▪ 081 838 41 11 ▪ Closed mid-Oct–mid-Apr ▪ www.jkcapri. com ▪ €€€

Standing proud above the port and painted white, this luxury villa with a private villa setting and elegant rooms makes a conscious effort to recall the island's ancient heritage – this spot is where the Emperor Tiberius had one of his villas. There is private access to a small beach as well as a heated outdoor swimming pool. Breakfast is included.

Villa Sarah

MAP U1 ▪ Via Tiberio 3/A ▪ 081 837 78 17 ▪ Closed Nov–Mar ▪ www.villasarahcapri.it ▪ €€€

Located up towards Villa Jovis (see p34) from the busy centre of Capri, this beautifully converted old villa is a bucolic retreat with a lovely garden and a small pool. The hotel's hillside position affords spectacular views of the island and the sea.

Sorrentine Peninsula Sojourns

Hotel La Primavera, Massa Lubrense

MAP D5 ▪ Via IV Novembre 3G ▪ 081 878 91 25 ▪ www.laprima vera.biz ▪ €

This restaurant-hotel, perched on a rocky spur, enjoys great views and is surrounded by lush olive groves.

La Tonnarella, Sorrento

MAP D5 ▪ Via Capo 31 ▪ 081 878 11 53 ▪ Closed Nov–Mar ▪ www.la tonnarella.it ▪ €

With its clifftop setting and elegant interiors, this is an amazing find. Guests can enjoy the pleasant private beach and a good restaurant in a wonderful glass-walled setting with panoramas of the bay. Book in advance.

Mega Mare

MAP D5 ▪ Corso Caulino 74 ▪ 081 802 8494 ▪ www.hotelmegamare. com ▪ €

Set high on the cliffside between Vico Equense and Meta, this simple but well-maintained hotel offers breathtaking views of the peninsula. Facilities include a fine swimming pool and a continental breakfast buffet included within the price.

Nice, Sorrento

MAP D5 ▪ Corso Italia 257 ▪ 081 878 16 50 ▪ www.hotelnice sorrento.com ▪ €

Small, simply furnished, and located near the Campania region, this modest hotel is just a few blocks from the main square of Sorrento.

For a key to hotel price categories see p126

Piccolo Paradiso, Massa Lubrense

MAP D5 ▪ Piazza Madonna della Lobra 5, Marina di Lobra ▪ 081 878 92 40 ▪ www.piccolo-paradiso. com ▪ €

A simple yet well laid-out family-run hotel with a lovely pool, sun terrace and stunning sea views.

Bellevue Syrene, Sorrento

MAP D5 ▪ Piazza della Vittoria 5 ▪ 081 878 10 24 ▪ www.bellevue.it ▪ €€€

Built on the ruins of a 2nd-century BC Roman villa, this pretty hotel with a view carries the Roman theme forward with Pompeian decor in some rooms and even a Jacuzzi that has been made to resemble a Roman bath.

Grand Hotel Excelsior Vittoria, Sorrento

MAP D5 ▪ Piazza Tasso 34 ▪ 081 877 71.11 ▪ www. exvitt.it ▪ €€€

Historic and utterly beautiful, with its clifftop position, extensive well-manicured gardens and grounds, and lavish public and private spaces. One of the world's best.

Hotel Capo La Gala, Vico Equense

MAP D4 ▪ Via Luigi Serio 8, Scrajo ▪ 081 801 57 57 ▪ www.capolagala.com ▪ Open Apr–Oct ▪ €€€

In a stunning spot along the Sorrentine Coast, this resort is hewn out of the living rock. There are only 22 rooms, each with a sea view and guests have access to sulphur baths, a private beach and a Michelin-starred gourmet restaurant, Il Maxi.

Imperial Hotel Tramontano, Sorrento

MAP D5 ▪ Via Veneto 1 ▪ 081 878 25 88 ▪ Closed Jan–mid-Mar ▪ www. hoteltramontano.it ▪ €€€

This is another fabulous property, built on top of a Roman villa, and frequented by the great and regal. Guests have included Romantic poets Shelley and Byron. A pool, gardens and striking panoramas render it as unforgettable today as it was in Grand Tour times.

La Medusa, Castellammare di Stabia

MAP E4 ▪ Via Passeggiata Archeologica 5 ▪ 081 872 33 83 ▪ www.lamedusa hotel.com ▪ €€€

This grand country villa has an array of elegant touches, from terracotta vases adorning the gate, to the busts of Roman emperors, as well as gardens, fountains and a pool. Rooms are spacious and the dining is superb.

Amalfi Coast Stays

Lidomare, Amalfi

MAP E4 ▪ Largo Piccolomini ▪ 089 87 13 32 ▪ www.lidomare.it ▪ €

A charming, family-run *pensione*, not far from the seaside, with large, airy rooms, tiled floors and antique furniture.

Villa Maria, Ravello

MAP E4 ▪ Via Trinità 14 ▪ 089 85 72 55 ▪ www. villamaria.it ▪ €€

This atmospheric villa offers cooking courses and boasts one of the best restaurants in town. There are superb vistas from the foyer.

Belmond Hotel Caruso, Ravello

MAP E4 ▪ Piazza San Giovanni del Toro 2 ▪ 089 85 88 01 ▪ Closed Nov–Feb ▪ www.hotelcaruso.com ▪ €€€

Housed in a beautiful 11th-century palace, touches of its original splendour abound. The view of the coastline from the infinity pool is breathtaking.

Il San Pietro, Positano

MAP E5 ▪ Via Laurito 2 ▪ 089 87 54 55 ▪ www. ilsanpietro.it ▪ €€€

This five-star hotel is just east of Positano proper in an isolated spot. No fewer than 20 terraces, hewn out of the rock, feature individual guest rooms with private balconies and Jacuzzis. A lift takes guests down to the foyer from the car park, and a second lift delivers you to the private beach, but you'll have to take the steps to reach the tennis court.

Le Sirenuse, Positano

MAP E5 ▪ Via Cristoforo Colombo 30 ▪ 089 87 50 66 ▪ Closed Nov–Mar ▪ www.sirenuse.it ▪ €€€

A palatial establishment decorated in signature Amalfi Coast style, with vibrant majolica tiles and antiques. There is a small pool, a gym, and the hotel restaurant is renowned.

Luna Convento, Amalfi

MAP E5 ▪ Via Pantaleone Comite 33 ▪ 089 87 10 02 ▪ www.lunahotel.it ▪ €€€

This former convent has a unique position at one end of Amalfi, clinging to a cliff, with a fortified tower on the promontory that is now used for special events. The rooms are tiny but charming, and the pool is a big draw.

Monastero Santa Rosa, Conca dei Marini

MAP E5 ▪ Via Roma 2 ▪ 089 832 11 99 ▪ Closed Nov– Mar ▪ www.monastero santarosa.com ▪ €€€

Situated at the edge of a cliff overlooking the coastline, this former convent has been exquisitely transformed into a luxurious retreat, complete with a terraced garden, spa and infinity pool. The refined decor is in keeping with the historic atmosphere and secluded setting.

Palazzo Avino, Ravello

MAP E4 ▪ Via S Giovanni del Toro 28 ▪ 089 81 81 81 ▪ www.palazzoavino.com ▪ €€€

Opened in 1997 in a 13th-century palace, the decor is a ravishing blend of Moorish and European elements. Other highlights include incredible views, a fabulous restaurant and a beach club.

Palumbo Palazzo Confalone, Ravello

MAP E4 ▪ Via S Giovanni del Toro 16 ▪ 089 85 72 44 ▪ www.hotelpalumbo.it ▪ €€€

The 12th-century Palazzo Confalone has been converted into one of the area's finest hotels. Its fine architecture reveals Arabic and Oriental influences, and many of its columns are ancient Greek and Roman. The service is impeccable, while the views and the restaurant are unsurpassed.

Santa Caterina, Amalfi

MAP E5 ▪ Strada Amalfitana 9 ▪ 089 87 10 12 ▪ Closed Nov–Mar ▪ www.hotelsanta caterina.it ▪ €€€

Amalfi's finest hotel is perched on a clifftop above the town. Its beautifully appointed rooms and "honeymoon" suites are airy and decorated with antique furniture. Gardens, a pool, a lift to the private beach and two restaurants add to the overall luxury.

Villa Cimbrone, Ravello

MAP E4 ▪ Via Sta Chiara 26 ▪ 089 85 74 59 ▪ www. villacimbrone.com ▪ €€€

Inimitably captivating with its frescoed ceilings, priceless antiques and amazing views and gardens.

Island Charmers

Il Monastero, Ischia

MAP A4 ▪ Castello Aragonese, Ischia Ponte ▪ 081 99 24 35 ▪ Closed Nov–mid-Apr ▪ www. albergoilmonastero.it ▪ €

This hotel occupies part of the monastery of the Castello itself. Consequently the rooms are quite basic, but the views are prized. There is also a well-maintained garden on the premises.

Ischia hotel: Hotel Ulisse

MAP B4 ▪ Via Champault 9, Ischia Porto ▪ 081 991737 ▪ Closed Oct–Mar ▪ www.hotelulisse. com ▪ €

Friendly, good-value hotel with charming, tiled rooms, and pretty gardens that surround a pair of pools. Great views of the castle from the rooftop terrace.

Hotel Crescenzo, Procida

MAP B4 ▪ Marina della Chiaollella 33 ▪ 081 896 72 55 ▪ www.hotel crescenzo.it ▪ €

This little hotel is known as much for its excellent fish restaurant as for its accommodation. Some of the rooms give direct access onto the harbour.

Villa Angelica, Ischia

MAP A4 ▪ Via IV Novembre 28, Lacco Ameno ▪ 081 99 45 24 ▪ www.villa angelica.it ▪ €

A sunlit setting, hospitality and Mediterranean architecture is what greets you upon arrival. It has a spa, and the sea is on your doorstep.

La Casa sul Mare, Procida

MAP B4 ▪ Salita Castello 13, Corricella ▪ 081 896 87 99 ▪ Closed Nov–Feb ▪ www.lacasasulmare.it ▪ €€

Housed in a renovated building dating from 1700, this hotel is at the foot of the acropolis of Terra Murata. Most rooms enjoy views of the picturesque fishing village.

Miramare e Castello, Ischia

MAP A4 ▪ Via Pontano 5, Ischia Ponte ▪ 081 99 13 33 ▪ www.miramaree castello.it ▪ €€

The premium rooms here have balconies with bay vistas, but all accommodation is on the beach and in sight of the Castello Aragonese. Other pluses include elegant public areas and lots of facilities – a spa and beauty centre, a private beach, and two swimming pools, one with thermal water.

For a key to hotel price categories see p126

Procida Hotel Terramurata

MAP B4 ▪ Via San Michele 9 ▪ 081 896 93 85 ▪ Closed Nov–Mar ▪ www. terra murata.it ▪ €€

A charming, tiny B&B set high on the hill above both Corricella and Marina Grande, with brightly-lit rooms, friendly hosts and great views over the sea.

Villa Marinella, Ischia

MAP A4 ▪ Via Castiglione 66, Casamicciola Terme ▪ 091 842 07 54 ▪ www. villamarinellaischia.it ▪ €€

This elegant B&B with large and attractive, individually-decorated rooms is ideally located between the main ports of the island, Ischia Porto and Casamicciola Terme, and is also close to the thermal parks.

Albergo Regina Isabella and Royal Sporting, Ischia

MAP A4 ▪ Piazza S Restituta 1, Lacco Ameno ▪ 081 99 43 22 ▪ www. reginaisabella.it ▪ €€€

This hotel may have been at its best in the 1950s, but it still has a charming air of sophistication. In a good location overlooking the sea, facilities include a swimmming pool jutting out over the beach and spa services.

Il Moresco Grand Hotel, Ischia

MAP A4 ▪ Via E Gianturco 16, Ischia Porto ▪ 081 98 13 55 ▪ www.ilmoresco.it ▪ €€€

The Neo-Moorish architecture, the spa and the careful service have made this hotel the meeting point of an international clientele. Situated in the most beautiful corner of

the island, the refined villa is set in a lush green park surrounding a thermal pool, and is just a few steps away from its own private beach.

Agriturismos, Villas and B&Bs

Agriturismo La Ginestra, Vico Equense

MAP D4 ▪ Via Tessa 2, Santa Maria del Castello ▪ 081 802 32 11 ▪ www. laginestra.org ▪ No air conditioning ▪ €

The farm's organically grown produce tempts most guests to sign on for half-board. The farmhouse has airy rooms, many of which have good views down to the sea.

Agriturismo La Pergola

MAP A4 ▪ Via San Giuseppe 24 ▪ 081 90 94 83 ▪ www.agriturismo lapergola.it ▪ €

Homely residence set amid vineyards and olive trees. Windows overlook the courtyard and provide gorgeous views over the sea. Rooms are spacious and tidy and the meals are delicious.

Agriturismo Le Grotelle, Sorrento

MAP D5 ▪ Via Zatri 3 ▪ 081 808 53 93 ▪ www. agriturismosorrentole grotelle.com ▪ €

Peaceful farmhouse in the hills south of Sorrento offering a pair of simple rooms equipped with private terraces that overlook the Sorrento Peninsula. Guests enjoy homecooked meals and participate in the owners' production of olive oil and cheese.

Casa Cosenza, Positano

MAP E5 ▪ Via Trara Genoino 20 ▪ 089 87 50 63 ▪ www.casacosenza.it ▪ €

A sunny B&B run by a local family, Casa Cosenza stands halfway down the Positano hillside, offering stunning views from its tiled terrace. The rooms vary – some have a balcony or private terrace; all have en-suite bathrooms. Apartments are also available.

Il Giardino di Vigliano, Massa Lubrense

MAP D5 ▪ Località Villazzano ▪ 081 533 98 23 ▪ www.vigliano.org ▪ €

The name originates from Roman times, as does the site, and the panorama inspires poets even to this day. Lemon groves abound, their fragrance adding a sweet note to the air of total relaxation on offer at this villa.

Residence La Neffola, Sorrento

MAP D5 ▪ Traversa Capo I 3 ▪ 081 878 13 44 ▪ www. neffolaresidence.com ▪ €

"Neffola" is the name of a fresh spring coming out of the rocks outside the town of Sorrento. his charming building has been restored and is surrounded by lovely gardens.

Hotel Punta Chiarito, Ischia

MAP A4 ▪ Via Sorgeto 51, Forio ▪ 081 90 81 02 ▪ Closed Nov–Mar ▪ www.puntachiarito.it ▪ €€

Given its spectacular position, it is not at all surprising that guests refer to the place as a paradise. It is surrounded by colourful and fragrant vegetation while a natural source of thermal water fills basins created with local stone.

Il Roseto Resort, Sorrento

MAP D5 ▪ Corso Italia 304 ▪ 081 878 10 38 ▪ www.ilrosetosorrento.com ▪ €€
Complete with a lush lemon-tree grove and a pool, this family-run B&B offers a comfortable stay not far from the centre of Sorrento. The rooms have views overlooking the sea or the garden.

Hostels and Camping

Agorà Hostel

MAP E4 ▪ Via Duca d'Aosta 15/19 ▪ 081 058 28 26 ▪ www.agorapompei.com ▪ €
Conveniently located between the train station and the centre of Pompeii, this air-conditioned hostel has a dormitory and few simple rooms set around a pleasant, shaded courtyard. The staff is friendly.

Ave Gratia Plena

MAP F4 ▪ Via dei Canali ▪ 089 234 776 ▪ www.ostellodisalerno.it ▪ €
Clean dorms and doubles set within the airy cloister of an old church near the centre of Salerno's old town.

Beata Solitudo, Agerola

MAP E5 ▪ Piazza Avitabile 4 ▪ 081 802 50 48 ▪ www.beatasolitudo.it ▪ €
Friendly and excellent value hostel and campground high in the hills above Amalfi.

Camping La Caravella

MAP B4 ▪ Via IV Novembre 2 ▪ 081 810 11 75 ▪ www.campingla caravella.blogspot.com ▪ No air conditioning ▪ €
Well-run camp grounds with helpful, welcoming hosts, set within easy reach of supermarkets and Chiaia beach.

Camping Zeus, Pompeii

MAP E4 ▪ Via Villa dei Misteri 3 ▪ 081 861 53 20 ▪ www.campingzeus.it ▪ No credit cards ▪ No air conditioning ▪ €
Located close to the archaeological site, within the grounds of this verdant camp site you'll find a bar, a restaurant and shops. For those who prefer not to be under canvas, there are also bungalows for rent.

Hostel A' Scalinatella, Atrani

MAP E5 ▪ Piazza Umberto I 5–6 ▪ 089 87 14 92 ▪ www.hostelscalinatella.com ▪ No credit cards ▪ No air conditioning ▪ €
In this family-run operation there are dormitory rooms with private bathrooms, and apartments scattered all over town, up and down the staircases that serve as streets here.

Hostel Brikette, Positano

MAP E5 ▪ Via G Marconi 358 ▪ 089 87 58 57 ▪ www.brikette.com ▪ €
Decorated with mosaic tiles and the owner's murals, this hostel offers friendly and helpful service. A variety of rooms are available, including those with en-suite bathrooms

and sea views. It is near a bus stop but a bit of a hike up from the beach.

Hostel delle Sirene, Sorrento

MAP D5 ▪ Via degli Aranci 160 ▪ 081 807 29 25 ▪ www.hostellesirene.net ▪ €
This self-proclaimed "VIP backpacker" establishment is the best deal in town. Although short on views, it's convenient enough to everything of importance, and is right behind the train station.

Nube d'Argento Camping, Sorrento

MAP D5 ▪ Via Capo 21 ▪ 081 878 13 44 ▪ www.nubedargento.com ▪ No credit cards ▪ No air conditioning ▪ €
A camp site that enjoys views of Vesuvius. Facilities include pools and a restaurant.

Ring Hostel

MAP A4 ▪ Via Gaetano Morgera 72 ▪ 081 997 531 ▪ www.ringhostel.com ▪ €
Welcoming hostel set in an old monastery, with a communal rooftop terrace. Ring Hostel offers frequent excursions to Il Sorgeto.

Vulcano Solfatara Camping, Pozzuoli

MAP C3 ▪ Via Solfatara 161 ▪ 081 526 74 13 ▪ www.campeggio vulcanosolfatara.it ▪ €
Services here include a bar, a swimming pool, and a restaurant. For exploring Naples, this is the best camp site in the area, located conveniently near a metro stop and the port of Pozzuoli for island trips in the area, as well. There are also independent bungalows for rent.

General Index

Acknowledgments

Author

American-born Jeffrey Kennedy now lives mainly in Italy and Spain. A graduate of Stanford University, he divides his time between producing, acting and writing. He is the co-author of Top 10 Rome and the author of the Top 10 guides to Mallorca, Miami and the Keys, San Francisco and Andalucia.

Additional Contributor
Laura Thayer

Publishing Director Georgina Dee

Publisher Vivien Antwi

Design Director Phil Ormerod

Editorial Michelle Crane, Rachel Fox, Ruth Reisenberger, Sally Schafer, Sophie Wright

Cover Design Bess Daly, Maxine Pedliham

Design Tessa Bindloss, Richard Czapnik

Commissioned Photography Demetrio Carrasco, Rough Guides/Karen Trist, Clive Streeter

Picture Research Susie Peachey, Ellen Root, Lucy Sienkowska, Oran Tarjan

Cartography Subhashree Bharti, Tom Coulson, Fabio Ratti Editoria, Suresh Kumar, James MacDonald

DTP Jason Little

Production Olivia Jeffries

Factchecker Alessandra Pugliese

Proofreader Leena Lane

Indexer Helen Peters

First edition created by Blue Island Publishing, London

Revisions Team
Avanika, Parnika Bagla, Alice Fewery, Bharti Karakoti, Shikha Kulkarni, Meghna, Vinita Venugopal

Picture Credits

The publisher would like to thank the following for their kind permission to reproduce their photographs:
Key: a-above; b-below/bottom; c-centre; f-far; l-left; r-right; t-top

123RF.com: Jennifer Barrow 87tl; perseomedusa 113cl.

4Corners: SIME/Massimo Borchi 47cl, /Pietro Canali 55cr, 65b, /Antonio Capone 61cl, /Demma 72tl, /Giovanni Simeone 58tl.

Alamy Stock Photo: age fotostock/Christian Goupi 44tl, /Pietro Scozzari 72bl; AGF Srl Antonio Capone 46cl, 69clb, 73bl; Jennifer Barrow 4crb, 61tr; Giuseppe Bartuccio 71tr; Mark Bassett 4cr; blickwinkel 2tr, 40-1; Bon Appetit/Alexandra Grablewski 93crb; Massimiliano Bonatti 85bl; Massimo Buonaiuto 78br; Julia Catt Photography 28tl; Robin Chapman 67br; Richard Cummins 14br; Collection Dagli Orti 53cra;

Design Pics Inc /Richard Cummins 15cr; Adam Eastland 27tl, 83cra; Elenaphotos 106cla; FC_ Italy 29tr; Peter Forsberg / Shopping 69tr; GL Archive 20tr; Granger, NYC. 42tc; hemis.fr/ Camille Moirenc 98-9, /Ludovic Maisant 13tr, 13cr, /René Mattes 59tl, 108tr; Heritage Image Partnership Ltd/Fine Art Images *Maria Amalia of Saxony], Queen of Naples* by Bonito, Giuseppe 96cra; John Heseltine 30cl; imageBROKER/ Bahnmueller 114bl, /Erich Schmidt 59br; Lebrecht Music and Arts Photo Library/*The Sicilian Vespers* by Barabino 42b; MARKA/ Massimiliano Bonatti 93cla; Barry Mason 4b; Mayday 58b; nagelestock.com 1; PAINTING/ National Museum of Capodimonte, Naples/ *Judith Slaying Holofernes* by Artemisia Gentileschi 22br; Pacific Press/Emanuele Sessa 73tr; REDA &CO srl/Alfio Giannotti 38bc; Francesca Sciarra 6br; Eugene Sergeev 100c; Sites & Photos/Capture Ltd 18crb; Stock Italia 33clb; The Art Archive/Collection Dagli Orti 4clb; Ivan Vdovin 11tl, 22r, 29cl, 48t, 96bl; Visions of America, LLC/Joseph Sohm 56-7; Christine Webb 81cra, 83bl; World History Archive 51tr; Ernst Wrba 68bl, 71cl.

AWL Images: Demetrio Carrasco 58cr.

Bowinkel: Uberto Bowinkel 91tl.

Bridgeman Images: Look and Learn 43cl.

Corbis: Atlantide Phototravel/Massimo Borchi 34cl; Bettmann 33crb; Design Pics/Jon Spaull 84cra; Leemage 18-9, 78cla; Tuul & Bruno Morandi 52tl; Ocean/68/Buena Vista Images 66cl; SOPA/Kaos02 54b, 111tl.

Da Paolino Lemon Trees: 109bl.

Dreamstime.com: Adreslebedev 11br; Agneskantaruk 67cl; Alexchered 62cl; Amoklv 36-7; Leonid Andronov 11crb, 14-5c; Baloncici 46b; Jennifer Barrow 30-1, 54cla; Beriliu 10cra; Vincenzo De Bernardo 61tl; Ciolca 49c, 105cb; Wessel Cirkel 32br, 94cla, 95br; Conde 45cl; Dennis Dolkens 12-3; Elen 44b; Faberfoto 36clb; Fedecandoniphoto 69tl; Sergii Figurnyi 102cla; Freesurf69 4t; Frenta 2tl, 8-9; Janos Gaspar 24-5, 102br, 37crb; Gigavisual 38-9; Giuseppemasci 27crb; Francesco Riccardo Iacomino 3tl, 74-5; Vladimir Korostyshevskiy 20bl, 26cla, 26br, 73cl, 86cla, 87br; Lachris77 10cl, 88b; Leonardoboss 101tr; Lukaszimilena 7tl; Rosario Manzo 3tr, 10br, 116-7; Mariyasiyanko 115crb; Merlin1812 33tl; Milosk50 112tr, 114cl; minnystock 4cla, 27-6, 103tl; MNStudio 68c, 81cb; Danilo Mongiello 112cla, 39tl; Anna Pakutina 76tl; Photogolfer 10c, 77tl, 80t; Enrico Della Pietra 16cl, 88tl; Angela Ravaioli 112bl; Reidlphoto 4cl; Michele Renzullo 31cb; Sarra22 12bl, 23cb; Scaliger 11cra, 60bl, 70br, 14cl; Oleksii Skopiuk 16-7b, 17cb; Slasta20 66tr; Smilemf 7clb; Andrei Stancu 34crb; Dariusz Szwangruber 11c, 34-5; Ttatty 111br; Vacclav 95t; Cinar Yilancioglu 60t; Tetiana Zbrodko 35clb.

Getty Images: De Agostini Picture Library 18cla, 22cl, 33tr, /Archivio J. Lange 10clb, /A. Dagli

Orti19br; Lonely Planet 92bl; Mondadori Portfolio 28b; Sergio Anelli/Electa /Mondadori Portfolio 23tl; UIG/Leemage 21clb; Peter Unger 30crb; Eric Vandeville 32cl.

Mamamu: 82tr.

Milleunaceramica: 106bc.

Museo MADRE, Naples: *Axér / Desaxér* (2015) by Daniel Buren, photo Amedeo Benestante 63tl.

Museo Nazionale Ferroviario di Pietrarsa: Giuseppe Senese 64bl.

Museobottega della Tarsialignea: 48bc.

Ospedale delle Bambole: Roberto Jandoli 65cr.

Photo Scala, Florence: courtesy of Curia Vescovile di Napoli 16-7; DeAgostini Picture Library 17tl, /Sammlungen des Fuersten von Liechtenstein, Vaduz, Liechtenstein/ *Portrait of the Royal Family of Naples. Ferdinand IV of the Two Sicilies (Naples, 1751-1825) and his Wife Maria Carolina of Austria (1752-1814) with their Sons* (1783) by Angelica Kauffmann 43br; Fondo Edifici di Culto - Min. dell'Interno 50tl; courtesy of the Ministero Beni et Att. Culturali 19tc, 28c, / Museo di San Martino, Naples/*Gratitude for ceasing the plague* by Gargiulo, Domenico (called Micco Spadaro 1612-1679) 43tl, Certosa di San Martino, Naples/ *Triumph of Judith* by Luca Giordano 51cl.

President Restaurant: 97cr.

Rex by Shutterstock: Courtesy Everett Collection 52cr, 52bl; imageBROKER 12cr, 62br; Miramax/Everett 53cla; Paramount/Everett 53bl; UIG/ Photoservice Electa 50br.

Robert Harding Picture Library: Charles Bowman 26-7c; Peter Barritt 21tr; Helmut Corneli 70t; Alfio Giannotti 110cla; Olivier Goujon 37tc; Arco Images GmbH/R. Kiedrowski 34bc; R. Kiedrowski 107tr; Ivan Vdovin 45tr; Ernst Wrba 14crb.

Teatro Bellini: 90crb.

Cover

Front and spine: **iStockphoto.com:** Cheryl Ramalho.

Back: **AWL Images:** ClickAlps cla; **Dreamstime. com:** Frenta crb, Janos Gaspar tr, Yi Liao tl; **iStockphoto.com:** Cheryl Ramalho bc;.

Pull Out Map Cover

iStockphoto.com: Cheryl Ramalho

All other images © Dorling Kindersley
For further information see:
www.dkimages.com

As a guide to abbreviations in visitor information blocks: **Adm** *= admission charge;* **D** *= dinner;* **L** *= lunch.*

MIX
Paper from
responsible sources
FSC™ C018179
www.fsc.org

Printed and bound in China

First edition 2004

Published in Great Britain by
Dorling Kindersley Limited
80 Strand, London WC2R 0RL

Published in the United States by
DK Publishing, 345 Hudson Street,
New York, New York 10014

Copyright © 2004, 2019 Dorling Kindersley Limited

A Penguin Random House Company

18 19 20 21 10 9 8 7 6 5 4 3 2 1

Reprinted with revisions 2006, 2008, 2010, 2012, 2014, 2016, 2019

A CIP catalogue record is available from the British Library.

A catalog record for this book is available from the Library of Congress.

ISSN 1479-344X

ISBN 978-0-2413-6178-8

SPECIAL EDITIONS OF DK TRAVEL GUIDES

DK Travel Guides can be purchased in bulk quantities at discounted prices for use in promotions as premiums. We also offer special editions and personalized jackets, corporate imprints, and excerpts from all of our books, tailored specifically to meet your own needs.

To find out more, please contact:

in the US
specialsales@dk.com
in the UK
travelguides@uk.dk.com
in Canada
specialmarkets@dk.com
in Australia
penguincorporatesales@ penguinrandomhouse.com.au

Phrase Book

yellow	**giallo**	*jal-loh*
green	**verde**	*vair-deh*
blue	**blu**	*bloo*

In an Emergency

Help!	**Aiuto!**	*eye-yoo-toh*
Stop!	**Ferma!**	*fair-mah*
Call a doctor	**Chiama un medico**	*kee-ah-mah oon meh-deekoh*
Call an ambulance	**Chiama un' ambulanza**	*kee-ah-mah oon am-boo-lan-tsa*
Call the police	**Chiama la polizia**	*kee-ah-mah lah pol-ee-tsee-ah*
Call the fire brigade	**Chiama i pompieri**	*kee-ah-mah ee pom-pee-air-ee*

Communication Essentials

Yes/No	**Sì/No**	*see/noh*
Please	**Per favore**	*pair fah-vor-eh*
Thank you	**Grazie**	*grah-tsee-eh*
Excuse me	**Mi scusi**	*mee skoo-zee*
Hello	**Buongiorno**	*bwon jor-noh*
Goodbye	**Arrivederci**	*ah-ree-veh-dair-chee*
Good evening	**Buona sera**	*bwon-ah sair-ah*
What?	**Che?**	*keh*
When?	**Quando?**	*kwan-doh*
Why?	**Perchè?**	*pair-keh*
Where?	**Dove?**	*doh-veh*

Useful Phrases

How are you?	**Come sta?**	*koh-meh stah*
Very well, thank you.	**Molto bene, grazie.**	*moll-toh beh-neh grah-tsee-eh*
Pleased to meet you.	**Piacere di conoscerla.**	*pee-ah-chair-eh dee coh-noh-shair-lah*
That's fine.	**Va bene.**	*va beh-neh*
Where is/ are…?	**Dov'è?/ Dove sono…?**	*dov-eh/ doveh soh-noh*
How do I get to…?	**Come faccio per arrivare a…?**	*koh-meh fah-cho pair arri-var-eh a*
Do you speak English?	**Parla inglese?**	*par-lah een-gleh-zeh*
I don't understand.	**Non capisco.**	*non ka-pee-skoh*
I'm sorry.	**Mi dispiace.**	*mee dee-spee-ah-cheh*

Shopping

How much does it cost?	**Quant'è, per favore?**	*kwan-teh pair fah-vor-eh*
I would like…	**Vorrei…**	*vor-ray*
Do you have…?	**Avete…?**	*ah-veh-teh*
Do you take credit cards?	**Accettate carte di credito?**	*ah-chet-tah-teh kar-teh dee creh-dee-toh*
What time do you open/close?	**A che ora apre/ chiude?**	*a keh ora ah-preh/ kee-oo-deh*
this one	**questo**	*kweh-stoh*
that one	**quello**	*kwell-oh*
expensive	**caro**	*kar-oh*
cheap	**economico**	*ee-con-om-ee-coh*
size (clothes)	**la taglia**	*lah tah-lee-ah*
size (shoes)	**il numero**	*eel noo-mair-oh*
white	**bianco**	*bee-ang-koh*
black	**nero**	*neh-roh*
red	**rosso**	*ross-oh*

Types of Shop

bakery	**il forno/ panificio**	*eel forn-oh/ panee-fee-coh*
bank	**la banca**	*lah bang-kah*
bookshop	**la libreria**	*lah lee-breh-ree-ah*
cake shop	**la pasticceria**	*lah pas-tee-chair-ee-ah*
chemist	**la farmacia**	*lah far-mah-chee-ah*
delicatessen	**la salumeria**	*lah sah-loo-meh-ree-ah*
department store	**il grande magazzino**	*eel gran-deh ma-gad-zeenoh*
grocery	**alimentari**	*ah-lee-men-tah-ree*
hairdresser	**il parrucchiere**	*eel par-oo-kee-air-eh*
ice-cream parlour	**la gelateria**	*lah jel-lah-tair-ree-ah*
market	**il mercato**	*eel mair-kah-toh*
newsstand	**l'edicola**	*leh-dee-koh-lah*
post office	**l'ufficio postale**	*loo-fee-choh pos-tah-leh*
supermarket	**il supermercato**	*eel su-pair-mair-kah-toh*
tobacconist	**il tabaccaio**	*eel tah-bak-eye-oh*
travel agency	**l'agenzia di viaggi**	*lah-jen-tsee-ah dee vee-ad-jee*

Sightseeing

art gallery	**la pinacoteca**	*lah peena-koh-teh-kah*
bus stop	**la fermata dell'autobus**	*lah fair-mah-tah dell-ow-toh-booss*
church	**la chiesa/ basilica**	*lah kee-eh-zah bah-seel-ee-kah*
closed for holidays	**chiuso per ferie**	*kee-oo-zoh pair fair-ee-eh*
garden	**il giardino**	*eel jar-dee-no*
museum	**il museo**	*eel moo-zeh-oh*
railway station	**la stazione**	*lah stah-tsee-oh-neh*
tourist information	**l'ufficio del turismo**	*loo-fee-choh del too-ree-smoh*

Staying in a Hotel

Do you have any vacant rooms?	**Avete camere libere?**	*ah-veh-teh kah-mair-eh lee-bair-eh*
double room	**una camera doppia**	*oona kah-mairah doh-pee-ah*
with double bed	**con letto matrimoniale**	*kon let-toh mah-tree-moh-nee-ah-leh*
a room with bath/ shower	**una camera con bagno/ doccia**	*oona kah-mair-ah kon ban-yoh/ dot-chah*
twin room	**una camera con due letti**	*oona kah-mairah kon doo-eh let-tee*

| single room | una camera singola | oona kah-mairah sing-goh-lah |
| I have a reservation | Ho fatto una prenotazione | oh fat-toh oona preh-not-tsee-oh-neh |

Eating Out

Have you got a table for…?	Avete un tavolo per…?	ah-veh-teh oon tah-voh-loh pair
I'd like to reserve a table	Vorrei prenotare un tavolo	vor-ray pre-noh-ta-reh oon tah-voh-loh
breakfast	colazione	koh-lah-tsee-oh-neh
lunch	pranzo	pran-tsoh
dinner	cena	cheh-nah
the bill	il conto	eel kon-toh
waitress	cameriera	kah-mair-ee-air-ah
waiter	cameriere	kah-mair-ee-air-eh
fixed-price menu	il menù a prezzo fisso	eel meh-noo ah pret-soh fee-soh
dish of the day	piatto del giorno	pee-ah-toh dell jor-no
starter	l'antipasto	lan-tee-pass-toh
first course	il primo	eel pree-moh
main course	il secondo	eel seh-kon-doh
vegetables	i contorni	ee kon-tor-noh
dessert	il dolce	eel doll-cheh
wine list	la lista dei vini	lah lee-stah day vee-nee
glass	il bicchiere	eel bee-kee-air-eh
bottle	la bottiglia	lah bot-teel-yah
knife	il coltello	eel kol-tell-oh
fork	la forchetta	lah for-ket-tah
spoon	il cucchiaio	eel koo-kee-eye-oh

Menu Decoder

l'acqua minerale	lah-kwah meenair-ah-leh	mineral water
gassata/ naturale	gah-zah-tah/ nah-too-rah-leh	fizzy/ still
agnello	ah-niell-oh	lamb
aglio	al-ee-oh	garlic
al forno	al for-noh	baked
alla griglia	ah-lah greel-yah	grilled
la birra	lah beer-rah	beer
la bistecca	lah bee-stek-ah	steak
il burro	eel boor-oh	butter
il caffè	eel kah-feh	coffee
la carne	la kar-neh	meat
carne di maiale	kar-neh dee mah-yah-leh	pork
la cipolla	la chip-oh-lah	onion
il formaggio	eel for-mad-joh	cheese
le fragole	leh frah-goh-leh	strawberries
il fritto misto	eel free-toh mees-toh	mixed fried seafood
la frutta	la froot-tah	fruit
frutti di mare	froo-tee dee mah-reh	seafood
i funghi	ee foon-ghee	mushrooms
i gamberi	ee gam-bair-ee	prawns
il gelato	eel jel-ah-toh	ice cream

l'insalata	leen-sah-lah-tah	salad
il latte	eel laht-teh	milk
il manzo	eel man-tsoh	beef
l'olio	loh-lee-oh	oil
il pane	eel pah-neh	bread
le patate	leh pah-tah-teh	potatoes
le patatine fritte	leh pah-tah-teen-eh free-teh	chips
il pepe	eel peh-peh	pepper
il pesce	eel pesh-eh	fish
il pollo	eel poll-oh	chicken
il pomodoro	eel poh-moh-dor-oh	tomato
il prosciutto cotto/ crudo	eel pro-shoo-toh kot-toh/ kroo-doh	ham cooked/ cured
il riso	eel ree-zoh	rice
il sale	eel sah-leh	salt
la salsiccia	lah sal-see-chah	sausage
il succo d'arancia	eel soo-koh dah-ran-chah	orange juice
il tè	eel teh	tea
la torta	lah tor-tah	cake/tart
l'uovo	loo-oh-voh	egg
vino bianco	vee-noh bee-ang-koh	white wine
vino rosso	vee-noh ross-oh	red wine
lo zucchero	loh zoo-kair-oh	sugar
la zuppa	lah tsoo-pah	soup

Time

one minute	un minuto	oon mee-noo-toh
one hour	un'ora	oon or-ah
a day	un giorno	oon jor-noh
Monday	lunedì	loo-neh-dee
Tuesday	martedì	mar-teh-dee
Wednesday	mercoledì	mair-koh-leh-dee
Thursday	giovedì	joh-veh-dee
Friday	venerdì	ven-air-dee
Saturday	sabato	sah-bah-toh
Sunday	domenica	doh-meh-nee-ka

Numbers

1	uno	oo-noh
2	due	doo-eh
3	tre	treh
4	quattro	kwat-roh
5	cinque	ching-kweh
6	sei	say-ee
7	sette	set-teh
8	otto	ot-toh
9	nove	noh-veh
10	dieci	dee-eh-chee
11	undici	oon-dee-chee
17	diciassette	dee-chah-set-teh
18	diciotto	dee-chot-toh
19	diciannove	dee-cha-noh-veh
20	venti	ven-tee
30	trenta	tren-tah
40	quaranta	kwah-ran-tah
50	cinquanta	ching-kwan-tah
60	sessanta	sess-an-tah
70	settanta	set-tan-tah
80	ottanta	ot-tan-tah
90	novanta	noh-van-tah
100	cento	chen-toh
1,000	mille	mee-leh

Selected Naples Street Index